★★★ TAKE ME ★★★ OUT TO THE BALL GAME

COMICAL AND FREAKISH
INJURIES WE CANNOT MAKE UP

DAVE BERGER

Publication date: October 2020

ISBN Print: 978-1-7352967-0-8
ISBN eBook: 978-1-7352967-1-5

Library of Congress Control Number: 2020915764

1. Baseball   2. Injuries   3. Statistics   4. Fun Facts   5. Careers   6. Hall of Fame
I Berger, Dave.   II *Take Me Out To The Ballgame*

Take Me Out To The Ballgame may be purchased at special quantity discounts for giveaways, fundraising, or sales promotions for Baseball Teams at all levels. For right and licensing agreements, special branded printings, or to have Dave speak at your event contact him: daveberger@att.net 512-825-1895

Cover and Interior Layout and Design: Megan Leid
Editor: Mel Cohen
Proofreader: Tracy Johnson
Publishing Consultant: Mel Cohen of Inspired Authors Press LLC
inspiredauthorspress.com
Publisher: Baseball Injury Publishers
Website: http://www.baseballinjurybook.com
Printed in the United States of America

This work depicts actual events in the life of the Major League Baseball Players as truthfully as our research permits and/or can be verified by print and online verifications through the 2019 season. All persons within are actual individuals; there are no composite characters.

"As a former professional ballplayer, a student of the game, and a lifelong baseball fan I really enjoyed reading this book. I have not come across another publication like it. It will surprise & entertain you with details about current and your all-time favorite players. It was certainly a fun read."

—Val Majewski
Rutgers University 1999-2002
Played professionally from 2002-2012
Baltimore Orioles: 2004
Houston, Los Angeles Angels, Oakland and Texas organizations

"I thoroughly enjoyed reading this book. If you are interested in quirky sports stories, then this book will suit you! It was a quick read full of interesting tidbits about America's favorite pastime."

—Jon Berger
San Diego State University: 2007-2009
San Diego Padres Organization: 2009-2010

"Entertaining and enjoyable anecdotes. A great job of sharing some of baseball's lighter moments. Baseball fans across the spectrum should thoroughly enjoy this book."

—Gregg Miller
Round Rock Express, Triple Affiliate Houston Astros

"Stories of when super humans become very human. Entertaining to the last!"
—Ryan Kjos
University of Texas: 1992-95
Oakland A's Organization:1995-1998

"Dave Berger's handling of some awfully funny and ironic anecdotes provides readers with a nice little peek through the windows of ballplayers lives on and off the field. I especially liked the referral to "David Cone's Mother in Law, now ex-Mother in Law." In its totality, this work reminds us that these grown men, in so many ways remain children at heart, even though they've made a huge public splash in the strangely intriguing world of the perspiring arts."

—Mike Capps
Published author and Voice of the Round Rock Express
www.cappspbp.com

ACKNOWLEDGEMENTS

This idea of this book first came about in July of 2010. And the proverb really is true that a desire accomplished is sweet to the soul. You know when the creator of the universe lives in your heart through his son Jesus Christ, you get His ideas and His inspiration and that was certainly true for this book. Last December, I wrote in my journal; II Corinthians 8:10-11, which reads, "And in this I give advice: It is to your advantage not only to be doing what you began and were desiring to do a year ago; but now you also must complete the doing of it; that as there was a readiness to desire it, so there also may be a completion out of what you have."

From that point on, this project got the legs it needed to and starting walking. Thank you Lord for putting the ideas, the format, and the stories which all came together to create the book you are about to read!

Thank you to my wife, Ruby, who is the kindest person I have ever met. My thought was that I had to get this book finished before I got married, but it was the opposite in that by having the honor to get married to you, this book got finished. I'm glad all my typing was able to put you to sleep at night…maybe there is a second or third book out there so my typing can put you to sleep in the future. Thank you for holding me accountable in finishing this because there were times when you asked me what I was doing, when the typing stopped. One I vividly remember was watching a YouTube video on a fight that George Brett got into verses writing about George Brett! Love ya babe!

To my dad, who wrote the Foreword to this book; little did we know 10 years to the month that as we discussed someone's injury, we mentioned that a book should be written about them. Thanks for forwarding me a bunch of these stories; a lot of them made it to the book.

To my brother, Ross, who also forwarded numerous stories to me and provided many true baseball stories he experienced on his own, some you couldn't make up! Hopefully, we can play together in the outfield again soon.

To my mom, who knew writing ran in our family?

To Mel, my publishing consultant, thank you for your patience, your expertise, and advice on what will work, what wouldn't, and there is no such thing as a "half-bad" idea; it's either a good idea or a great idea. I hope you had as much fun editing this book and managing the process as I had in putting these stories together. Here's hoping that your Phillies and my Indians meet in the World Series soon.

To Megan and Tracy for expertise on the book layout and editing. I thought my grammar wasn't half bad but that was blown out of the water. Thank you for making this first-class!

To Jon, Val, Gregg, Mike, and Ryan for taking time to provide endorsements for this book. Appreciate your time and feedback and the love of baseball that we all share.

To Vicky, Mandy, Jamie and Jay: it's been an absolute joy to be a part of you and your families' lives.

To Andrew, Jaren and Jordyn; thanks for asking me how my book is coming and indirectly pushing me to get this done; Andrew, thanks for the tip on AJ Burnett, as the Pirates were the last team I needed.

To all the readers that will read this book that I will never meet. Thank you for taking the time to read this and if you chuckled or thought to yourself, I never knew that, then the book accomplished what I desired.

CONTENTS

FOREWORD

It has been stated thousands of times that baseball is the greatest game ever created. Baseball is a game that has been passed down from generation to generation. The season ends with one team lifting the World Series Championship trophy. Excitement reigns with game winning walk off home runs. Excitement reigns when a starting pitcher hasn't given up a base hit through eight innings. Excitement reigns when a batter hits a triple and slides safely into third base, beating the relay throw from the outfield.

For every game winning hit, an injury can occur to a different player. A player is interviewed about his game winning hit while the injured player is being worked on in the trainer's room. Is the injury serious enough that would result in the injured player going on the injured list? That is the question the injured player is concerned with.

Injuries can occur at any moment. Former rookie of the year and Cleveland Indians pitcher Herb Score was hit in the eye by a line drive off the bat of Gil McDougald on May 7, 1957. McDougald was the second batter in the game. Fans weren't even settled in their seats yet. Score was lost for the season with broken facial bones and an injured eye.

Injuries can occur in spring training, before the start of the regular season, on the field, or off the field. Indians player Ken "Hawk" Harrelson broke his leg sliding into second base during an exhibition game on March 19, 1970. He was limited to 17 games that season. His injured leg contributed to his retirement from baseball.

Injuries can occur to high-salaried free agent players. The Indians signed pitcher Wayne Garland to a ten-year contract for $2,300,000 following the 1976 season when free agency for players was just beginning. Garland suffered a torn rotator cuff injury in his second year with the Indians. He struggled on the mound for three seasons after surgery to repair his rotator cuff. He pitched only five seasons with the Indians before retiring from baseball while the Indians paid him for five more seasons to honor his ten-year contract even though Garland was retired.

I have been a season ticket holder of the Cleveland Indians since 1993. I have seen good baseball, lousy baseball, thrilling games, lopsided losses, walk off home runs, both for the Indians and their opponents. I have witnessed injuries like those suffered by Herb Score, Ken Harrelson and Wayne Garland. I have seen freak injuries, many of which are contained in this book.

Baseball is a serious game; an intense battle between pitcher and batter, as well as the manager trying to out-wit the opposing manager. Occasionally an injury occurs that simply defies logic. Many of these off the wall injuries are recalled in this book. Sit back, relax and enjoy the replay of some of the funniest baseball injuries that you will ever come across.

Glenn Berger

Cleveland Indians

Here is why I'm not pitching Game 2.

TREVOR BAUER

Pitcher, Cleveland

What: "Fear the Drone"

Where: His home

When: 10/17/16

Story: Indians pitcher Trevor Bauer suffered an unusual injury to his finger while repairing a drone, ahead of the biggest start of his MLB career.

As he plugged in his drone, the propellers started turning at full speed and sliced his pinkie finger. Bauer was supposed to start in Game 2 of the ALCS, but that was pushed back to Game 3 because he needed stitches.

What the heck is he thinking? The biggest start in his career on the horizon and he's playing with his drone?

Who doesn't like playing with drones? It seems every Christmas, my son Andrew gets a drone which usually lasts a week or two before it's broken, caught in a tree, or flies out of range to be lost forever.

Well, at least when we plugged ours in, the power was off because as Bauer plugged in his drone, the propellers turned on at full speed, sliced his pinkie finger, and knocked him out of the biggest start of his career!

Wasn't surprised to learn that Trevor collects drones.

MLB Debut: 6/28/12

Teams played for: Arizona, Cleveland, and Cincinnati

Career Stats: 70-60, 4.04 ERA, 1,179 K

Fun Fact: In 2018, along with Corey Kluber, Carlos Carrasco and Mike Clevinger, Cleveland became the first pitching staff to have 4 starters each record over 200 strikeouts.

KYLE DENNEY
Pitcher, Cleveland

Look mom, I can explain.

What: Those boots were made for walking and being bulletproof

Where: Kansas City

When: September 2004

Story: Not sure if the Tribe stopped this hazing ritual after this story, but we're sure they made some modifications to their shenanigans. Poor Kyle was coerced into wearing a cheerleading outfit, complete with a pair of boots. As the team bus made its way from the stadium to the airport, Denney was shot by a stray bullet. Trainers had to remove the bullet from his calf; police mentioned in their investigation that the boots he had on lessened the impact of the bullet.

MLB Debut: 9/14/04

Last MLB appearance: 9/29/04

Career Stats: 1-2, 9.56 ERA, 13 K

Teams played for: Cleveland

BOB FELLER
Pitcher, Cleveland

What: Hold onto that hose

Where: Training room

When: 1951

Story: Feller scalded himself with 200-degree water after he lost control of the hose in a whirlpool. He scalded himself from the waist down and couldn't do anything for a week.

MLB Debut: 7/19/36

Last MLB appearance: 9/30/56

Career stats: 266-152, 3.25 ERA, 2,581 K

Teams played for: Cleveland

First-ballot Hall of Famer–1962

Accolades: 8 times All-Star, World Series champion (1948), Triple Crown–1940 (led league in wins, strikeouts and ERA), 6 times AL wins leader, AL ERA leader (1940), 7 times MLB strikeout leader, pitched three no-hitters and had 12 one-hitters.

Fun Fact: Signed as a 16-year old after his sophomore year in high school for one dollar and an autographed baseball.

Fun Fact #2: Feller's catcher in high school was Nile Kinnick, the 1939 Heisman Trophy winner.

Fun Fact #3: In his major league debut, struck out the first three batters he faced.

Fun Fact #4: Became the first pitcher to win 24 games before the age of 21.

Fun Fact #5: Threw the only Opening Day no-hitter in major league history in 1940.

Fun Fact #6: After the bombing of Pearl Harbor became the first American professional athlete to enlist in the armed services.

This is right out of the story of Roy Hobbs in The Natural: The Indians brought him to the majors in 1936 at the tender of age 17 right off the Iowa farm. He struck out 15 in his first major league start. A few starts later he fanned 17 to set the American League record. That made him one of the most famous players in the country—and he hadn't even graduated from high school yet. In fact, when he finished up high school that winter, NBC Radio covered his graduation. How about that for a send-off from Iowa!

EARL AVERILL
Center Field, Cleveland

What: Do as I say, not as I do

Where: Averill casa

When: 6/28/35

Story: Averill's 673 consecutive game streak came to an abrupt end while showing the four little Averills what not to do. It seems as he was lighting firecrackers, one exploded while he was holding it, and he suffered lacerations on his right fingers as well as burns on his face and chest. After several weeks he made a full recovery and was ready to start a new consecutive game streak, which did not last 673 games.

MLB Debut: 4/16/29

Last MLB appearance: 4/25/41

Career Stats: .318, 238 HR, 1,164 RBI

Teams played for: Cleveland, Detroit, Boston

Home plate has to be down there somewhere!

Accolades: 6 times All-Star

Fun Fact: Hit a home run in his first major league at bat.

Fun Fact #2: On 9/17/30, became the first player to hit four home runs in a doubleheader.

Fun Fact #3: He famously hit a line drive that broke Dizzy Dean's foot in the 1937 All-Star game, which led to Dean changing his pitching motion, and in turn, damaging his arm and retiring at the age of 31, four years later.

Fun Fact #4: At times, insisted on flying with his bat in a gun case.

Fun Fact #5: His son, Earl D., also played in the big leagues from 1956-1963.

CHRIS JOHNSON
First Baseman, Cleveland

What: That bug will bite!

Where: Minneapolis

When: 8/17/15

Story: Raise your hand if you've told your kids, "Watch out, sleep tight, don't let the bed bugs bite." Johnson would definitely agree with that. He was forced out of the lineup on Saturday and Sunday because of a suspected bite from a spider at a hotel in Minneapolis. Seemed it swelled up on him; he had his hand wrapped and was put on antibiotics.

MLB Debut: 9/9/09

Last MLB appearance: 10/2/16 (one day after his 32nd birthday)

Teams played for: Houston, Arizona, Atlanta, Cleveland, Miami

Career Stats: .275, 63 HR, 339 RBI, 773 H

BRIAN GILES
Outfield, Cleveland

What: Arachnophobia!

Where: Unknown

When: 1998 season

Story: Giles was forced to sit out several games during the 1998

campaign after he sustained several spider bites. The bites were so severe that Giles required shots of antibiotics in order to recover.

MLB Debut: 9/16/95

Last MLB appearance: 6/18/09

Career Stats: .291, 287 HR, 1,078 RBI

Teams played for: Cleveland, Pittsburgh, San Diego

Accolades: 2 times All-Star

SANDY ALOMAR JR.
Catcher, Cleveland

What: You're 6'5", Sandy, buy a truck for long road trips

Where: Cleveland

When: 1994

Story: The author (Dave Berger) worked at a nightclub in downtown Cleveland as a valet and had the pleasure of driving Alomar's sports car. The only problem with that is that Alomar drove the same car to spring training in Florida, which was 1,082 miles. When he got to Florida, he had a very sore back.

MLB Debut: 9/30/88

Last MLB appearance: 9/30/07

Career Stats: .273, 112 HR, 588 RBI

Teams played for: San Diego, Cleveland, Chicago White Sox, Colorado, Chicago White Sox, Texas, Los Angeles Dodgers, Chicago White Sox, New York Mets

Accolades: AL Rookie of the Year (1990), Gold Glove Award (1990), 6 times All-Star

Fun Fact: Is the first catcher in major league history to start an All-Star game and win Rookie of the Year as well as a Gold Glove.

Fun Fact #2: Third catcher in history, besides Carlton Fisk and Johnny Bench, to win a Gold Glove in his rookie year.

Kansas City Royals

BRIAN FLYNN

Pitcher, Kansas City

What: Gravity wins every time

Where: His barn

When: February 2017

Story: This is a classic! Before heading off to spring training, Brian had some household chores that needed to be done. This included getting on top of his barn to do what farmers do on top of the barn, which this city slicker is completely unaware. It seems Flynn lost his footing, fell through the roof, and landed on some hay, which did not prevent a re-entry injury. Flynn suffered a broken rib and 3 fractured vertebrae and missed 8 weeks.

Flynn is a lefty.

MLB Debut: 9/4/13

Teams played for: Miami, Kansas City

Career Stats: 6-12, 4.41 ERA, 134 K

GEORGE BRETT

Third Base, Kansas City

What: Breaks bone on door jamb

Where: His home

When: 6/7/83

Story: On a rare day off in 1983, Royals slugger George Brett was at home doing laundry with the Cubs game playing in another room. When he heard the announcers say that one of his favorite players, Bill Buckner, was coming up to the plate, Brett rushed to get in front of the TV.

The only problem was that he wound up slamming his foot into the door jamb on his way—breaking his toe and landing on the disabled list.

***It should be noted that previously Brett was more infamously known for leaving Game 2 of the 1980 World Series game with a case of hemorrhoids.

MLB Debut: 8/2/73

Last MLB appearance: 10/3/93

Teams played for: Kansas City Royals

Career Stats: .305, 317 HR, 1,596 RBI, 3,154 H

Accolades: 13 times All-Star, World Series Champion (1985), AL MVP (1980), ALCS MVP (1985), Gold Glove Award (1985), 3 times Silver Slugger Award, 3 times AL batting champion.

First-ballot Hall of Famer–1999

Fun Fact: Only player to win a batting title in 3 different decades

Fun Fact #2: Got a base hit in his last at bat

Fun Fact #3: After his 3,000th hit, got picked off 1st base enjoying the moment.

Really, I'm a Hall of Famer and you pick me off?

Fun Fact #4: Brett named one of his sons after Robin Yount, who was inducted into the Hall of Fame the same year he was, in 1999.

Fun Fact #5: He won his first batting title in 1976 with a .333 average. The four contenders for the batting title that year were Brett and Royals teammate Hal McRae and Minnesota Twins teammates Rod Carew and Lyman Bostock. In dramatic fashion, Brett went 2 for 4 in the final game of the season against the Twins, beating out McRae, Carew and Bostock all playing in the same game. His lead over second-place McRae was less than .001. Brett won the title when a fly ball dropped in front of the Twins left-fielder and bounced on the Royals Stadium AstroTurf and over his head to the wall. Brett circled the bases for an inside-the-park home run. McRae, batting just behind Brett in the line-up, grounded out and thus giving Brett his first batting title.

Fun Fact #6: Only player in history to have 3,000 hits, 300 home runs, 600 doubles, 100 triples, 1,500 RBI, and 200 steals

Fun Fact #7: Google George Brett and 7/24/83 and you'll be highly entertained.

SALVADOR PEREZ
Catcher, Kansas City

What: Who put bricks in this suitcase?

Where: Perez home

When: March 2018

Story: Kansas City will be without Salvador Perez for up to six weeks after the star catcher sprained the medial collateral in his left knee while carrying a suitcase up some stairs in his home. Apparently Perez slipped and injured his knee. No surgery is required, and recovery can be as little as four weeks. Sure, easy for the writer to say "as little as four weeks," he's not the one who has to recuperate. The freak injury left the Royals without one of their top hitters when they opened the season against the White Sox. Perez hit .268 with career-bests of 27 homers and 80 RBIs last season.

MLB Debut: 8/10/11

Career Stats: .266, 141 HR, 503 RBI

Team: Kansas City

Accolades: World Series Champion (2015), World Series MVP, 6 times All-Star

LUIS AQUINO
Pitcher, Kansas City

What: Watch that plate

Where: Unknown Mexican restaurant

When: Early 1990s

Story: When the waitress tells you that this plate is hot, then you would tend to give her the benefit of the doubt, but not Luis. Upon his arrival of his oven-hot plate at a Mexican restaurant, he ignored the warnings of his server and touched it. This mishap resulted in a blister on his finger and he was scratched from a start.

MLB Debut: 8/8/86

Last MLB appearance: 9/12/95

Career Stats: 31-32, 3.68 ERA, 318 K

Teams played for: Toronto, Kansas City, Florida, Montreal, San Francisco.

Fun Fact: Member of the inaugural Florida Marlins in 1993.

MARK QUINN

Outfield, Kansas City

What: He's no Bruce Lee

Where: His home

When: February 2002

Story: Horse playing with brothers never gets old, but when we get older, recovering from those injuries can take longer than expected. Case in point with Quinn who was kung fu fighting with his brother and broke a rib when he fell backwards onto a chair. He opened the season on the disabled list and only appeared in 23 games that year in which would be his last year in the big leagues.

MLB Debut: 9/14/99

Last MLB appearance: 6/7/02

Career Stats: .282, 45 HR, 167 RBI

Teams played for: Kansas City

Fun Fact: One of only three players in major league history to hit two home runs in his major league debut.

Detroit Tigers

CAMERON MAYBIN
Outfield, Detroit

What: You're killin' me Cameron

Where: U.S. Cellular Park, Chicago

When: 6/13/16

Story: In honor of Buzz from Home Alone, make sure you: A, check the count on the scoreboard; 2, check with your first base coach; and D, do not ask the first baseman.

Maybin left Monday night's game against the Chicago White Sox in the fifth inning with an apparent injury after what turned out to be a needless headfirst slide into second base.

Maybin was trying to steal second base when Ian Kinsler took ball four on a 3-1 pitch from pitcher James Shields, meaning there was no play. The throw went to second base anyway, and when Maybin slid in, his slide jammed his left hand between the bag and second baseman Tyler Saladino's knee, bringing Maybin up in immediate pain. The trainer didn't need a long look before removing Maybin from the game.

MLB Debut: 8/17/07

Teams played for: Detroit, Florida Marlins, San Diego, Atlanta, Detroit, Los Angeles Angels, Houston, Miami Marlins, Seattle, New York Yankees

Career Stats: .256, 70 HR, 346 RBI, 183 SB

Accolades: World Series Champion (2017)

JOEL ZUMAYA
Pitcher, Detroit

What: Guitar hero overload

Where: His home

When: 2006

Story: During the 2006 season, Zumaya played so much of Guitar Hero that it caused a sore wrist, which in turn caused him to miss the 2006 ALCS. Fortunately for him, the Tigers beat the Oakland A's to advance to the World Series. He did pitch 3 games for the Tigers in the World Series, but Detroit lost to the St. Louis Cardinals in 5 games.

To his credit, the injury did get Zumaya recognition, albeit not recognition you would like. When Guitar Hero II came out, *Xbox 360* had the following message: No pitchers were harmed in making this game. Except for one. Joel Zumaya. He had it coming.

In addition to the above injury, in October 2007, Zumaya was in San Diego at his parent's house, moving boxes because of the California wildfires. As he was moving boxes of his World Series mementos, a heavy box fell off the shelf, hitting him in the shoulder and separating it.

MLB Debut: 4/3/06

Last MLB appearance: 6/28/10

Teams played for: Detroit

Career Stats: 13-12, 3.05 ERA, 210 K

Fun Fact: On 7/3/06, Zumaya, Justin Verlander, and Fernando Rodney each threw combined fastballs measured at over 100 mph, becoming the first time in MLB history that three pitchers on the same team had done so during a game.

DENNY McLAIN
Pitcher, Detroit

What: Toes dislocated

Where: Detroit

When: 9/18/67

Story: One night McLain went to bed completely healthy. The next day he woke up with four dislocated toes. The story goes that his foot fell asleep and he stubbed them—possibly sleep walking? Or was it caused by an organized crime figure stomping on his foot as punishment for failing to pay off a lost bet?

MLB Debut: 9/21/63

Last MLB appearance: 9/12/72

Career Stats: 131-91, 3.39 ERA, 1,282 K

Teams played for: Detroit, Washington, Oakland, and Atlanta

Accolades: 3 times All-Star, World Series and AL MVP (1968), 2 times Cy Young Award, 2 times AL wins leader

Fun Fact: Most recent of only 11 players to win 30 games in one year, going 31-6 in 1968. The last 30-game winner up to that point was Dizzy Dean who accomplished that feat in 1934.

Fun Fact #2: Married to Sharyn Boudreau, the daughter of former major league Hall of Famer Lou Boudreau.

Fun Fact #3: He picked off two baserunners and hit a home run in his major league debut, which was the only home run of his major league career. Since 1920, McLain is one of only 6 teenaged pitchers to hit a major league home run, a list that includes Hall of Famers Don Drysdale and Jim Palmer.

Fun Fact #4: In 1968, along with Bob Gibson of St. Louis, they became the first pitchers to win the MVP in both leagues.

Fun Fact #5: He appeared on a number of variety shows, where he was an accomplished organist, including The Ed Sullivan Show, The Steve Allen Show, and The Joey Bishop Show. He also released two albums.

Fun Fact #6: The last batter he faced was Pete Rose.

Fun Fact #7: He led the American League in home runs allowed in three consecutive years (1966-1968).

Funny story: McLain grew up admiring New York Yankee Mickey Mantle, who entered a game late in the 1968 season tied with Jimmie Foxx for third place in the major league home run list. McLain called his catcher out to the mound and had him tell Mantle he would be throwing only fastballs. Mantle, on the 3rd pitch, hit his 535th career home run, putting him sole possession of third place on the all-time home run list, behind Babe Ruth and Willie Mays. As Mantle rounded the bases, McLain stood on the mound and applauded. Mantle tipped his cap to McLain as he rounded the bases. The next batter, Joe Pepitone, waved his bat over the plate, as if asking for an easy pitch of his own. McLain responded by throwing the next pitch over Pepitone's head.

   ***Go to YouTube and type in Mickey Mantle and Denny McLain and you'll get Mantle's version of the story.

AL KALINE

Right field, Detroit

What: Careless Kaline

Where: Detroit

When: June 1967

Story: Normally mild mannered, Mr. Tiger lost his cool on a hot day in June. After striking out, which was a rarity, he smashed his bat into the bat rack. He ended up with a broken finger which caused him to miss 26 games. Four teams were battling for the pennant and with Kaline sidelined, the Tigers finished one game behind the Red Sox.

MLB Debut: 6/25/53

Last MLB appearance: 10/2/74

Career Stats: .297, 399 HR, 1,583 RBI, 3,007 H

Accolades: 18 times All-Star, World Series champion (1968), 10 times Gold Glove Award, AL batting champion (1955)

Teams played for: Detroit

First-ballot Hall of Famer–1980

Fun Fact: Came downstairs in his prom suit to sign his contract with the Tigers at the age of 16. From that point on he was under the employment by the Tigers for over 60 years.

Fun Fact #2: On 7/7/54, threw out a White Sox runner in three consecutive innings.

Fun Fact #3: Was the youngest player to ever win the American League batting title at age 20 in 1955.

Fun #4: Also in 1955, became the youngest player to hit three home runs in one game.

Fun Fact #5: Had more career walks (1,277) than strikeouts (1,020).

Fun Fact #6: First player to have his number retired by the Tigers.

BRANDON INGE
Third Base and Catcher, Detroit

What: Fluff twice, then drop it!

Where: Inge house

When: June 2018

Story: Inge was placed on the disabled list with a strained oblique. How did he strain his oblique, you might ask? By fluffing a pillow for his 3-year old daughter.

MLB Debut: 4/3/01

Last MLB appearance: 7/21/13

Teams played for: Detroit, Oakland, and Pittsburgh

Career Stats: .233, 152 HR, 648 RBI

Accolades: All-Star (2009)

Fun Fact: During the Home Run Derby in 2009, became the 8th player not to hit a single home run.

Chicago White Sox

CHRIS SALE

Pitcher, Chicago White Sox

What: That first step is a doozy

Where: Spring Training, Arizona

When: 2/27/15

Story: Suffered a foot injury in an accident at his home and would have to miss 3 weeks of preparation time for the regular season. Sale suffered a fracture to the side of his right foot at his spring training residence in Arizona. He initially declined to say how he injured it, but he came clean and admitted landing awkwardly when he got off the back of his truck while unloading items. Wonder if that was his honey do list.

Sale is a lefty.

MLB Debut: 8/6/10

Teams played for: Chicago White Sox, Boston

Career Stats: 109-73, 3.03 ERA, 2,007 K

Accolades: 2018 World Series Champion, 7 times All-Star, 2 times AL strikeout leader

Fun Fact: He is the fastest pitcher to record 1,500 strikeouts.

Fun Fact #2: Reached 2,000 strikeouts in the fewest innings (1,626) in MLB history.

CARLOS RODON

Pitcher, Chicago White Sox

What: Hippity hop to wearing a brace

Where: Chicago

When: July 2016

MLB Debut: 4/21/15

Story: Sprained his left wrist falling on the dugout steps. Rodon had to wear a brace for the next 7-10 days.

Rodon is a lefty.

MLB Debut: 4/21/15

Teams played for: Chicago White Sox

Career Stats: 29-31, 4.08 ERA, 519 K

MATT ALBERS
Pitcher, Chicago White Sox

What: This little piggy didn't go wee all the way home

Where: Chicago

When: 4/22/15

Story: You just never know what will occur when running in from the bullpen to break up and/or take part in a bench-clearing brawl between the White Sox and the Royals. White Sox placed Albers on the 15-day disabled list with a broken pinkie finger on his right hand.

MLB Debut: 7/25/06

Teams played for: Houston, Baltimore, Boston, Arizona, Cleveland, Houston, Chicago White Sox, Washington, Milwaukee

Career Stats: 47-48, 4.35 ERA, 571 K

FRANCISCO LIRIANO
Pitcher, Chicago White Sox

What: Scared kids over Christmas

Where: His home

When: December 2012

Story: 'Twas the night before Christmas and all through the house, not a creature was stirring, not even—well you know how the rest of the story goes. At the Liriano house, things happened to get a little more physical than reindeer landing on the roof, and after hearing this story, the kids had quite a memorable Christmas.

Francisco attempted to scare his kids by slamming his shoulder and breaking his arm (granted, it was his non-throwing arm), into a door. Not sure whether the kids were startled, but this ended up being a fairly expensive door; the stunt cost him $11 million dollars in guaranteed money!

Liriano is a lefty.

MLB Debut: 9/5/05

Teams played for: Minnesota, Chicago White Sox, Pittsburgh, Toronto, Houston, Detroit, Pittsburgh

Career Stats: 112-114, 4.15 ERA, 1,812 K

Accolades: All-Star (2006), World Series Champion (2017), 2 times Comeback Player of the Year (2010, 2013)

Fun Fact: Pitched a no-hitter 5/3/2011.

JERMAINE DYE
Right field, Chicago White Sox

What: That spider will bite

Where: Cleveland

When: July 2005

Story: This spider definitely had a bead on him as it bit Dye at a Cleveland hotel room which caused him to miss four games in the summer of 2005.

MLB Debut: 5/18/96

Last MLB appearance: 10/4/09

Career Stats: .274, 325 HR, 1,072 RBI

Team played for: Atlanta, Kansas City, Oakland, Chicago White Sox

Accolades: 2 times All-Star, World Series (2005), World Series

MVP, Gold Glove (2000)

Fun Fact: Hit a home run in his first major league at bat.

ROBERTO HERNANDEZ
Pitcher, Chicago White Sox

What: Down goes Ripken!

Where: Philadelphia

When: July 1996

Story: Hernandez's first All-Star game was quite an experience that he will tell his grandkids for a long time. As the American League was getting together for their team picture, Roberto slipped on the tarp, fell, and accidentally punched Cal Ripken, breaking Ripken's nose.

MLB Debut: 9/2/91

Last MLB appearance: 9/25/07

Career Stats: 67-71, 3.45 ERA, 945 K, 326 SV

Accolades: 2 times All-Star

Teams played for: Chicago White Sox, San Francisco, Tampa Bay, Kansas City, Atlanta, Philadelphia, New York Mets, Pittsburgh, New York Mets, Cleveland, Los Angeles

Fun Fact: His college baseball field at University of South Carolina-Columbia is named after him.

Fun Fact #2: One of eleven pitchers in major league history to appear in 1,000 career games.

CARLOS QUENTIN

Outfield, Chicago White Sox

What: Bye-bye MVP

Where: Cleveland

When: September 2008

Story: After fouling off a pitch, Quentin tried to tap his right hand on the bat as he was holding the bat with his left hand. This time the wrist tapped the bat, not his hand, which resulted in a fractured wrist. Quentin was done for the season. At the time of his injury he was an MVP candidate with 36 HR and 100 RBI.

MLB Debut: 7/20/06

Last MLB appearance: 7/26/14

Career Stats: .252, 154 HR, 491 RBI

Teams played for: Arizona, Chicago White Sox, San Diego

Accolades: 2 times All-Star, Silver Slugger Award (2008)

Minnesota Twins

MIGUEL SANO
Third Base and First Base, Minnesota

What: Rookie jitters

Where: Minnesota

When: 7/19/15

Story: Less than three weeks after making his major league debut, Miguel missed at least two games after spraining his right ankle stepping on a ball during infield drills.

MLB Debut: 7/2/15

Teams played for: Minnesota

Career Stats: .245, 118 HR, 315 RBI

TERRY MULHOLLAND
Pitcher, Minnesota

What: The pillow that bites

Where: Minnesota

When: 5/25/2005

Story: Where was My Pillow® when you need it?! He must have had a seamstress who wanted to get off early when she made those pillows that Mulholland slept on. He happened to wake up with a scratched eye from a loose feather that fell out of his pillow. Ouch.

It's safe to assume that there isn't a pillow in the Mulholland household that is stuffed with feathers today.

Mulholland is a lefty.

Teams played for: San Francisco, Philadelphia, New York Yankees, San Francisco, Philadelphia, Seattle, San Francisco, Chicago Cubs, Atlanta, Pittsburgh, Los Angeles Dodgers, Cleveland, Minnesota, Arizona

MLB Debut: 6/8/86

Last MLB appearance: 6/3/2006

Career Stats: 124-142, 4.41 ERA, 1,325 K

Accolades: All-Star (1993)

Fun Fact: Pitched a no-hitter on 8/15/90, the first no-hitter pitched in Veterans Stadium history.

Fun Fact #2: During his pitching career, he beat every major league team.

CARL PAVANO
Pitcher, Minnesota

What: Shoveling snow proven to be hazardous

Where: Pavano's house

When: January 2013

Story: Pavano had his spleen removed after the pitcher was injured when he fell in the snow shoveling his driveway. Hey Carl, after all that money the Yankees paid you, hire some kids to do that chore.

Teams played for: Montreal, Florida, New York Yankees, Cleveland, Minnesota.

There goes #70!

MLB Debut: 5/23/98

Last MLB appearance: 6/1/12

Career Stats: 108-107, 4.39 ERA, 1,091 K

Accolades: All-Star (2004)

World Series Champion (2003)

Fun Fact: Gave up Mark McGwire's 70th home run during the 1998 season.

RICK AGUILERA
Pitcher, Minnesota

What: Honey, need your help with my suitcase

Where: Spring Training

When: 1996

Story: Aguilera was going through a career change as he was transitioning from being a closer to being part of the rotation which was delayed when he hurt his wrist at the end of spring camp while unloading his wife's suitcase. There was something in the way he lifted the suitcase onto the truck with his right arm that gave him a severe case of tendinitis, which caused him to land on the disabled list to start the '96 season and miss the first six weeks of the season.

MLB Debut: 6/12/85

Last MLB appearance: 9/6/00

Career Stats: 86-81, 3.51 ERA, 1,030 K, 318 SV

Accolades: 3 times All-Star, 2 times World Series champion

Fun Fact: In Game 3 of the 1991 World Series, he became the first pitcher to pinch hit in a World Series game since Don Drysdale in 1965.

JASON BARTLETT
Shortstop, Minnesota

What: To get up or not get up?

Where: Hotel in Detroit

When: April 2004

Story: In town for a series against Detroit, and as a result of a snow out, Bartlett decided to stay in the hotel room and watch a basketball game on TV. As he tried to turn the TV to get a better angle, he got his fingernail caught underneath the TV and ripped it off.

MLB Debut: 8/3/04

Last MLB appearance: 4/6/14

Career Stats: .270, 31 HR, 286 RBI

Teams played for: Minnesota, Tampa Bay, San Diego, Minnesota

Accolades: All-Star (2009)

Fun Fact: On 7/23/99, made the final out in Mark Buehrle's perfect game.

DENNY HOCKING
Utility Positions, Minnesota

What: Watch where you celebrate

Where: Oakland

When: 10/6/02

Story: After catching the final out in the division series game against Oakland, Hocking was in the proverbial dog pile with his teammates. Well, while in that pile, he was spiked by one of his teammates, splitting his nail in two places. Because of that, he missed the entire ALCS.

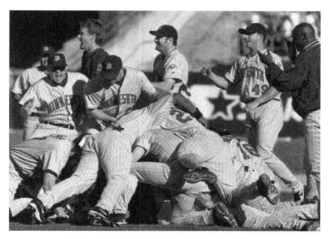

Come on guys, get off me!

MLB Debut: 9/10/93

Last MLB appearance: 9/28/05

Career Stats: .251, 25 HR, 226 RBI

Teams played for: Minnesota, Colorado, Kansas City

Fun Fact: While playing for the Twins in 2000, Hocking's wife gave birth to twins, which made him the first player in Twins franchise history to become the father of twins.

Fun Fact #2: Was a utility player his whole career, playing 7 of the 9 positions.

New York Yankees

JOBA CHAMBERLAIN
Pitcher, New York Yankees

What: Trampoline needs a net

Where: Tampa Bay

When: 5/22/12

Story: Well, those darn trampolines can be quite dangerous! This injury, while on the surface is humorous, turned out to be quite dangerous. As Chamberlain was playing with his son, he somehow slipped, fell, and broke his ankle so badly that a bone was sticking out through his skin! That is what they call an open dislocation! As the story goes, there was so much blood that many at the Tampa Jump Center thought it could have been life-threatening. Ouch.

MLB Debut: 8/7/07

Last MLB appearance: 7/3/16

Teams played for: New York Yankees, Detroit, Kansas City, Cleveland

Career Stats: 25-21, 3.81 ERA, 546 K

World Series Champion 2009

AARON BOONE
Infield, New York Yankees

What: Tore his knee up playing hoops

Where: Somewhere other than Yankee Stadium

When: January 2004

Story: You wonder why certain things are written into players'

contracts on activities they are not to do or risk their contract being voided. Well, Aaron learned this the hard way. Seemed he wanted to play a little hoops in the off-season to get some cardio in. The issue came up when he tore his knee pretending to be Woody Harrelson in *White Men Can't Jump*.

What did the Yankees decide to do? They released him on February 27, 2004.

***Now he's the skipper of the Yankees. He won 100 games in his first year as manager.

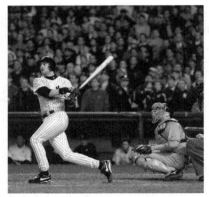

Who knew this would be my second to last hit as a Yankee?

MLB Debut: 6/20/97

Last MLB appearance: 10/4/09

Teams played for: Cincinnati, New York Yankees, Cleveland, Florida, Washington, Houston

Career Stats: .263, 126 HR, 555 RBI

Accolades: All-Star (2003)

Current manager of the New York Yankees (2018)

Fun Fact: Boone was ejected during the game he made his MLB debut in after being called out at home.

Fun Fact #2: On the final game of the 1998 season, the Reds started the only MLB infield with two sets of brothers: first baseman Stephen Larkin, second baseman Bret Boone, shortstop Barry Larkin, and third baseman Aaron Boone.

Fun Fact #3: On 9/22/02, Boone hit the last home run in Riverfront Stadium.

Fun Fact #4: He is descendant of pioneer Daniel Boone.

DAVID WELLS
Pitcher, New York Yankees—Story 1

What: You get what you deserve if you leave your car running

Where: San Diego

When: 1/12/97

Story: Whenever a story starts off with "A running car is left outside a bar," it can only go downhill from there. In San Diego to attend his mother's funeral, Wells decided to take his Lincoln Town Car to a bar; the issue was that he kept it running. Does that mean he was going there for a quick drink or was he drinking already? Maybe a little bit of both!

Two men walked up to the car, took the keys out of the ignition, and put them under the seat. Wells saw the men by his car and accused them of taking his keys, resulting in a shoving match between Wells, his friend, and the two men. Punches were thrown, and Wells landed a clean left to one man who slammed the back of his head into the ground and began to bleed. Wells was eventually cleared by the police but suffered a fractured left hand.

It should be noted that David was ready to go when the season began.

JOE DiMAGGIO
Center Field, New York Yankees

What: Say it ain't so, Joe

Where: Exhibition game

When: Spring 1936

Story: Joltin' Joe wasn't joltin' after this incident. During an exhibition game his foot was stepped on, and as a result of that his foot began to swell. He was given treatment that included placing the foot in a diathermy machine, where he was left unattended. How in the world does someone leave the Yankees number one prospect unattended? The heat control was not adjusted properly, burning his foot so badly that DiMaggio had to have two large blisters pricked; he then spent two days in the hospital. He ended up missing the first 16 games of his 1936 rookie season with first degree burns on his foot. He did make a nice comeback to hit .323 with 29 home runs and 125 RBIs.

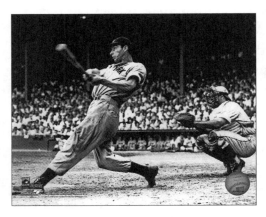

MLB Debut: 5/3/36

Last MLB appearance: 9/30/51

Career Stats: .325, 2,214 H, 361 HR, 1,537 RBI

Accolades: 13 times All-Star, 9 times World Series Champion, 3 times AL MVP, 2 times AL batting champion, 2 times AL home run leader, 2 times AL RBI leader

MLB record 56-game hitting streak in 1941; also hit safely in 61 games in the Pacific Coast League in 1933.

Fun Fact: Joe holds the record for most seasons with more home runs than strikeouts, a feat he accomplished 7 times.

Fun Fact #2: DiMaggio hit 148 home runs at home versus 213 on the road.

Fun Fact #3: After his 56-game hitting streak was over, he hit safely in the next 16 games. It's amazing that he hit safely in 72 out of 73 games.

DAVID CONE
Pitcher, New York Yankees

Sit....sit....sit....good dog.

What: Dog bite

Where: At home

When: June 1998

Story: Missed a start after getting bit by his mother-in-law's dog, Veronica. You would think with a name like Veronica, the dog would be a bit calmer. Ironically, Orlando (El Duque) Hernandez replaced Cone in the line-up and debuted in the big leagues.

***In 2011, she became his ex-mother-in-law.

MLB Debut: 6/8/96

Last MLB appearance: 5/28/03

Career Stats: 194-126, 3.46 ERA, 2,688 K

Teams played for: Kansas City, New York Mets, Toronto, Kansas City, Toronto, New York Yankees, Boston, New York Mets

Accolades: 5 times All-Star, 5 times World Series champion, AL Cy Young Award, MLB wins leader (1998), 2 times MLB strikeout leader.

Fun Fact: Pitched a perfect game on 7/18/99; it was the last shutout he would pitch in his career. On hand that day to watch the game was Yogi Berra and Don Larsen, who in 1956 were the catcher and pitcher in the only perfect game thrown in post-season history.

Fun Fact #2: He set the MLB record for most years between 20-win seasons with 10.

Fun Fact #3: In a well-known incident on 4/30/90, against the Atlanta Braves, Cone covered first base on a play, which should have retired the runner. Umpire Charlie Williams mistakenly ruled the runner safe. Arguing with Williams, and thinking time had been called, Cone held the ball while two Braves' runners scored.

HENRY COTTO
Outfield, New York Yankees

What: Keep your arms to yourself, senior

Where: Yankee Stadium

When: 1980s

Story: All Henry wanted to do was clean his ears with a Q-tip, only to have Ken Griffey Sr. bump into him. This shot the Q-tip into Cotto's ear, fracturing his ear drum. I bet Cotto didn't sit next to Griffey the rest of the year!

MLB Debut: 4/5/84

Last MLB appearance: 9/30/93

Career Stats: .261, 44 HR, 210 RBI

Teams played for: Chicago Cubs, New York Yankees, Seattle, Florida

Fun Fact: Played for the inaugural Florida Marlins in 1993.

RANDY KEISLER
Pitcher, New York Yankees

What: Snake bite

Where: His house

When: May 2002

Story: Keisler was already on the disabled list with a shoulder injury, and while he was recovering and gardening at his house he was bit by a pygmy rattlesnake. After that episode, if I were Keisler, I'd get a cat.

Keisler is a lefty.

MLB Debut: 9/10/00

Last MLB appearance: 7/27/07

Career Stats: 4-4, 6.63 ERA, 100 K

Teams played for: New York Yankees, San Diego, Cincinnati, Oakland, St. Louis

Boston Red Sox

CLARENCE BLETHEN
Pitcher, Boston

What: Dentures came back to bite Clarence, literally!

Where: On the field

When: 9/21/23

Story: Clarence spent 18 of his 19 years in minor leagues winning 257 games, which is very impressive. In 1923 he was called up to play with the big boys, the Boston Red Sox. He wore dentures and on that particular day, he thought he looked meaner if he took his false teeth out. Well, as he was sliding into 2nd base, the dentures clamped down on his posterior, taking such a big bite that he had to be removed from the game because of excessive bleeding.

This story gives new meaning to "That may come back to bite you." Who knows, maybe that is where this phrase came from.

Fun Fact: That was the only play he reached base in his big-league career.

MLB Debut: 9/17/23

Last MLB appearance: 9/26/29

Teams played for: Boston Red Sox, Brooklyn Robins

Career Stats: 0-0, 7.32 ERA, 2 K

WADE BOGGS
Third Baseman, Boston

What: Breaking in cowboy boots

Where: Toronto

When: 6/9/86

Story: Flirting with hitting .400 went out the window after this incident. Boggs tried to pry off his cowboy boots with his foot, only to lose his balance and fall rib-cage first into the arm of the couch. He ended up missing 6 games for not being able to take off his boots!

MLB Debut: 4/10/82

Last MLB appearance: 8/27/99

Teams played for: Boston, New York Yankees, Tampa Bay

Career Stats: .328, 118 HR, 1014 RBI, 1,412 BB, 3,010 H

Accolades: 12 times All-Star, World Series Champion (1996), 2 times Gold Glover, 8 times Silver Slugger Award winner, 5 times AL batting champion

First-ballot Hall of Famer–2005

Fun Fact: Along with Derek Jeter and Alex Rodriguez, they are the only players to get their 3,000th hit on a HR.

Fun Fact #2: He holds the record for the highest batting average at Fenway Park, at .369.

Fun Fact #3: Along with Cal Ripken (who played for the Rochester Red Wings), Boggs (who played for the Pawtucket Red Sox)

played in the longest game in professional baseball history in 1981; the game lasted 33 innings, over 8 hours covering two days.

Fun Fact #4: Hit the first home run in Tampa Bay Devil Rays history.

JAKE PEAVY
Pitcher, Boston

What: Full-contact fishing

Where: Fort Myers, Florida

When: February 2014

Story: Who knew an off day could be so dangerous. Jake goes out to fish and ends up cutting his non-throwing hand on a fishing knife. It could have been a lot worse as it almost cut through his left index finger.

It should be noted that after the Padres won the National League West in 2005, Peavy missed the rest of the season with a broken rib, which he apparently suffered while celebrating.

MLB Debut: 6/22/02

Last MLB appearance: 9/21/16

Career Stats: 152-126, 3.63 ERA, 2,207 K

Teams played for: San Diego, Chicago White Sox, Boston, San Francisco

Accolades: 3 times All-Star, 2 times World Series Champion, NL Cy Young (2007), 2 times MLB ERA leader, 2 times NL strikeout leader

Fun Fact: 9/17/04, Peavy surrendered Barry Bonds' 700th career home run.

Fun Fact #2: After the Giants defeated the Royals, 3–2 in Game 7 of the 2014 World Series, Peavy became the second starting pitcher in MLB history to win two consecutive World Series with two teams in two leagues.

BOB STANLEY
Pitcher, Boston

What: Take out the papers and the trash and don't come back!

Where: His house

When: January 1988

Story: It seems Stanley is not exempt from doing his share of honey do's, only this time it cost him a couple of games of his livelihood. Turns out that he slipped on some icy stairs taking out the trash and landed on a piece of glass, where several tendons and nerves were damaged to his pitching hand. After four hours of surgery, Stanley was on the mend. Ouch!

MLB Debut: 4/16/77

Last MLB appearance: 9/5/89

Career Stats: 115-97, 3.64 ERA, 693 K, 132 SV

Teams played for: Boston

Accolades: 2 times All-Star

Fun Fact: He is the Red Sox all-time leader in appearances with 637 and relief wins.

Fun Fact: #2: In 1979 became the only player in major league history born in Maine to be named to an All-Star game.

ROGER CLEMENS

Pitcher, Boston

What: Watch that finger, Roger

Where: Baltimore

When: 4/2/93

Story: After grabbing some grub, Clemens came across an injured terrier laying on the side of the road. Clemens got out of his car to help the dog, only to have it bite him on his right thumb. This prompted a trip to the ER to get a tetanus shot.

Maybe the dog was related to David Cone's mother-in-law.

MLB Debut: 5/15/84

Last MLB appearance: 9/16/07

Career Stats: 354-184, 3.12 ERA, 4,672 K

Teams played for: Boston, Toronto, New York Yankees, Houston, New York Yankees

Accolades: 11 times All-Star, 2 times World Series champion, 7 times Cy Young Award winner, AL MVP (1986)

Fun Fact: Won seven Cy Young awards during his career, more than any other hurler in history.

Fun Fact #2: In 2001 became the first pitcher in major league history to start a season with a win-loss record of 20-1.

Fun Fact #3: On 4/29/86 Clemens became the first pitcher in major league history to strike out 20 batters in a nine-inning game. He was the only pitcher to accomplish this twice.

Fun Fact #4: On 6/13/03 on my twin boys' first birthday, recorded his 300th career win and 4,000th career strikeout in the same game.

Fun Fact #5: Clemens is one of only three pitchers to pitch his entire career and reach 350 wins. One of the other two was Warren Spahn, whose catcher for his 350th win was Joe Torre. Torre was Clemens' manager for his 350th.

Toronto Blue Jays

DARRELL CECILIANI
Left Field, Toronto

What: Stretch before you come up to bat

Where: Atlanta, GA

When: 5/19/17

Story: Ceciliani smokes a 2-1 change-up over the wall in right field off Braves' pitcher Julio Teheran. As he hit the home run, he sustained a partial subluxation (a slight misalignment of the vertebrae) of the left shoulder, putting him on the 60-day disabled list. Hey, if you can't pronounce your injury, it's probably not a good thing!

What's ironic about this particular story was that this was his 2nd career home run!

MLB Debut: 5/19/15

Teams played for: New York Mets, Toronto

Career Stats: .190, 2 HR, 7 RBI

MICHAEL SAUNDERS
Outfield, Toronto

Come on honey, I can't pick up the groceries, look at me!

What: Look twice, step once

Where: Dunedin, FL

When: 2/25/15

Story: As Saunders was shagging fly balls, he inadvertently stepped on a sprinkler. This tore up his knee so much so that he was sidelined until the All-Star break.

MLB Debut: 7/25/09

Last MLB appearance: 10/1/17

Teams played for: Seattle, Toronto, Philadelphia, Toronto

Career Stats: .232, 570 H, 81 HR, 263 RBI

KEVIN PILLAR
Outfield, Toronto

What: Gesundheit!

Where: Dunedin, FL

When: Spring 2015

Story: Gesundheit: Which ironically, means "Good luck, God bless you."

Pillar sprained his oblique while getting into a sneezing fit. He felt a sharp pain in his side but decided not to tell trainers until the 5th inning of a spring training game. Hey, when you are fighting for a starting spot on your team, I'd keep my mouth shut as long as I could take it!

MLB Debut: 8/14/13

Teams played for: Toronto, San Francisco

Career Stats: .261, 640 H, 76 HR, 318 RBI, 69 SB

Fun Fact: Set the Division II record with a 55-game hitting streak in 2010

JOAQUIN BENOIT
Pitcher, Toronto

What: Stretch before you fight

Where: Toronto

When: 9/26/16

Story: Toronto Blue Jays reliever Joaquin Benoit missed the rest of the regular season after tearing his left calf muscle when he tripped and fell while running in from the bullpen. He wanted to be in the action during the second time the benches cleared. Toronto lost 7-5 to the Yankees.

Benoit left the stadium on crutches Monday and was still using them throughout the week. The team was optimistic that he would return before the start of the playoffs, but did not recover in time and missed the entire playoffs.

MLB Debut: 8/8/01

Last MLB appearance: 9/7/17

Teams played for: Texas, Tampa Bay, Detroit, San Diego, Seattle, Toronto, Philadelphia, Pittsburgh

Career Stats: 58-49, 3.83 ERA, 1,058 K, 53 SV

Fun Fact: Holds the MLB record for having recorded the longest save, seven innings, on 9/3/02, since it became an official stat in 1969.

Fun Fact #2: Benoit's injury kept him out of the 2016 playoffs, which helped my Tribe as they displaced the Blue Jays 4-1 to advance to the World Series.

RUSSELL MARTIN
Catcher, Toronto

What: Does anyone have an alarm clock?

Where: At his residence

When: June 2016

Story: An off-day trip to the health club knocked out Toronto catcher Russell Martin.

Martin felt "woozy" following an extended spell in the sauna at his Toronto residence. Martin injured his left knee when he passed out and fell while taking a cold shower. He missed several games.

"I woke up and I had the shower curtain half on my body, and the rest of my head was kind of sticking outside the shower," Martin said. "It's a weird feeling."

Fortunately, the MRI showed no structural damage. The four-time All-Star stated he may have aggravated an old injury.

Martin often treats soreness by alternating hot and cold water. He has felt "weak" before but never lost consciousness.

MLB Debut: 5/5/06

Last MLB appearance: 10/9/19

Teams played for: Los Angeles Dodgers, New York Yankees,

Pittsburgh, Toronto, Los Angeles

Career Stats: .248, 191 HR, 771 RBI, 1,370 H

Accolades: 4 times All-Star, Gold Glove Award (2007)

Fun Fact: Became the first ever Canadian born catcher to start an All-Star game.

Fun Fact #2: On 8/25/11, along with Robinson Canó and Curtis Granderson, Martin was one of the Yankees' three batters who hit an MLB record three grand slams in a single game.

BRETT CECIL
Pitcher, Toronto

What: Blender battle

Where: Boston

When: 9/16/11

Story: So much for helping a teammate out; apparently, the blender was left with food in it. Cecil stuck his hand into the blender to clean it out with four blades awaiting. With four blades, the chances of you cutting your hand shoot up quite dramatically as Cecil quickly found out. He cut his finger on one of the blades that was sticking up. Man, all the guy wanted was a protein shake, but instead he missed a start!

Brett Cecil, Act 2: It should be duly noted that he missed a spring training start in March 2010 when he cut his thumb while making chicken salad. Bet he doesn't mind getting take-out food.

Cecil is a lefty.

MLB Debut: 5/5/09

Teams played for: Toronto, St. Louis

Career Stats: 44-47, 4.29 ERA, 670 K

Accolades: All-Star (2013)

GLENALLEN HILL
Outfield, Toronto

Look mom, I'm not afraid anymore!

What: Spider dream

Where: His house

When: 1990

Story: As a member of the Toronto Blue Jays, Hill had a nightmare in which he was trying to escape from spiders. It was an escape that saw him fall down the stairs, bounce off the wall, and fall through a glass table. It resulted in multiple cuts and bruises and an eventual stay on the 15-day disabled list. How about that for a good morning. What came first? The cup of coffee or an Advil? This story was so far-fetched that Hill invited reporters over to take a look at his place to survey the damage that was done. From that point forward his nickname has been Spiderman.

MLB Debut: 7/31/89

Last MLB Appearance: 5/31/01

Teams played for: Toronto, Cleveland, Chicago Cubs, San Francisco, Seattle, Chicago Cubs, New York Yankees, Anaheim

Accolades: World Series Champion (2000)

Career Stats: .271, 186 HR, 586 RBI

Fun Fact: On 5/11/2000, Hill became the first player to hit a home run onto the five-story residential building across the street from Wrigley Field at 1032 W. Waveland Ave.

RICKEY HENDERSON
Left Field, Toronto

That's right, I'm thawing out my foot!

What: Frostbite in August?

Where: Training room

When: August 1993

Story: Seems Rickey needed a cat nap but forgot about the ice pack on his foot. He missed 3 games due to a case of frostbite in August!

MLB Debut: 6/25/79

Last MLB appearance: 9/19/03

Career Stats: .279, 3,055 H, 297 HR, 1,115 RBI, 1,406 SB, 2,295 R

Teams played for: Oakland, New York Yankees, Oakland, Toronto, Oakland, San Diego, Anaheim Angels, Oakland, New York Mets, Seattle, San Diego, Boston, Los Angeles Dodgers

Accolades: 10 times All-Star, 2 times World Series champion, AL MVP (1990), Gold Glove Award (1981), 12 times AL stolen base leader.

MLB records: 1,406 career stolen bases, 2,295 runs, 81 career lead-off home runs.

First-ballot Hall of Famer–2009

Fun Fact: In the history of Major League Baseball, only 57 position players are known to have only batted right and thrown left.

Fun Fact #2: In 1985, became the first player since Jimmie Foxx in 1939 to collect more runs scored than games played.

Fun Fact #3: Also in 1985, became the first player ever to reach 80 stolen bases and 20 home runs.

Fun Fact #4: On 8/22/89, Henderson became Nolan Ryan's 5,000th strikeout casualty.

Fun Fact #5: The last day of the 2001 season, which was Tony

Gwynn's final game, was just the second time in major league history that a pair of teammates each had over 3,000 hits.

Fun Fact #6: While leading off an inning, Henderson walked 796 times.

Fun Fact #7: Led off 81 games with a home run, which is a major league record.

HUCK FLENER
Pitcher, Toronto

What: Duck Huck!

Where: Airplane

When: Spring 1997

Story: On his way flying to Spring Training, Huck opened up the overhead bin only to have a briefcase drop on his shoulder, chipping his collarbone.

Huck is a lefty.

MLB Debut: 9/14/93

Last MLB appearance: 7/28/97

Career Stats: 3-3, 5.51 ERA, 55 K

Teams played for: Toronto

Accolades: World Series champion (1993)

Fun Fact: This is not a fun fact, but unfortunately Flener lost his right eye in 2001 on a ball hit back to him in the Venezuelan League.

Tampa Bay Rays

DAVID PRICE
Pitcher, Tampa Bay

What: The towel that snags

Where: Spring Training

When: 3/8/12

MLB Debut: 9/14/08

Story: Price suffered minor neck spasms after toweling himself too hard; this has been the 3rd time this has happened to him. Apparently, the towel catches the back of his head and pulls his neck forward. One would think that after the first time, you'd be a little wary of taking that towel to the back of the neck to dry out. Guess it took David three times to figure this out!

Teams played for: Tampa Bay, Detroit, Toronto, and Boston

Career Stats: 142-75, 3.25 ERA, 1,847 K

Accolades: 5 times All-Star, AL Cy Young Award (2012), AL wins leader (2012), 2 times AL ERA leader, MLB strikeout leader (2014), AL Comeback Player of the Year (2018) World Series Champion (2018)

RONALD BELISARIO
Pitcher, Tampa Bay

What: Slip-n-fall

Where: Venezuela

When: February 2015

MLB Debut: 4/7/09

Story: Belisario just couldn't seem to get out of his pool without fracturing his shoulder, granted, his non-throwing shoulder. But knowing you were going to camp without a roster spot guaranteed to him, you would think he'd be more careful. My guess is that there were adult beverages involved.

Teams played for: Los Angeles Dodgers, Chicago White Sox, Tampa Bay

Career Stats: 24-20, 3.85 ERA, 273 K

TAYLOR GUERRIERI
Pitcher, Tampa Bay

What: Fell out of bathtub

Where: Rental Home

When: March 2017

Story: Guerrieri needed stitches to close a cut near his right eyebrow after hitting his head on the bathtub of his rental home.

Guerrieri said he felt lightheaded and about to faint, so he braced himself but fell and hit his head on the corner of the tub. Guerrieri said he didn't know why he passed out—that he wasn't sick or dehydrated—and felt fine later. After the swelling went down, he got a couple of stitches.

MLB Debut: 9/1/18

Teams played for: Tampa Bay, Toronto, and Texas

Career Stats: 0-0 5.50 ERA, 35 K

CURT CASALI

Catcher, Tampa Bay

I'll never live this one down!

What: The first 90 feet is the hardest

Where: St. Petersburg, FL

When: 8/25/15

Story: Tampa Bay Rays catcher Curt Casali was placed on the 15-day disabled list one day after straining his left hamstring while running the bases after his home run in Tuesday night's 11-7 loss to Minnesota.

Casali's leg started getting tight en route to first base following his 10th homer in the fifth inning. He slowly finished his trip around the bases with a slight limp before heading toward the clubhouse.

So my questions are: What if he didn't hit a home run? Would this injury have never occurred? Or what if the home run didn't clear the fences and instead went off the wall? Would he have been thrown out at second base, as his running would have been impeded?

MLB Debut: 7/18/14

Teams played for: Tampa Bay, Cincinnati

Career Stats: .230, 31 HR, 97 RBI

JOEL PERALTA
Pitcher, Tampa Bay

What: Was the sandwich really worth it?

Where: Cuban Taste Restaurant, Port Charlotte

When: February 2013

Story: Peralta hurt his neck ducking out of his orange Camaro while stopping for sandwiches. Not just any sandwich, but Cuban sandwiches. Hope those sandwiches were worth it, because you know he was given a hard time about this at Spring Training. Bet he was not the one picked to go on any more sandwich runs! He couldn't throw for four days and to make matters worse, he had to withdraw from the World Baseball Classic.

MLB Debut: 5/25/05

Last MLB appearance: 7/5/16

Teams played for: Los Angeles Angels of Anaheim, Kansas City, Colorado, Washington, Tampa Bay, Los Angeles Dodgers, Seattle, Chicago Cubs

Career Stats: 20-35, 4.03, 612 K

ROCCO BALDELLI
Outfield, Tampa Bay

What: Say it ain't so, Rocco

Where: At his home in Rhode Island

When: November 2004

Story: While playing wiffle ball with his brother, he tore his left ACL and ended up missing the entire 2005 season.

MLB Debut: 3/31/03

Last MLB appearance: 10/3/10

Career Stats: .278, 60 HR, 262 RBI

Teams played for: Tampa Bay, Boston

Fun Fact: Became the youngest manager to win the American League manager of the year for the Minnesota Twins in 2019 at the age of 38.

Baltimore Orioles

UBALDO JIMENEZ
Pitcher, Baltimore

What: Sprained right ankle

Where: Parking lot

When: June 2014

Story: Jimenez's miserable season worsened when the Baltimore Orioles right-hander was placed on the 15-day disabled list with a sprained right ankle.

Jimenez twisted his ankle in a parking lot at his apartment complex. Rumor had it that he was playing catch with a football.

MLB Debut: 9/26/06

Last MLB appearance: 9/22/17

Teams played for: Colorado, Cleveland, and Baltimore

Career Stats: 114-117, 4.34 ERA, 1,720 K

Accolades: All-Star (2010)

Fun Fact: Pitched a no-hitter as a member of the Colorado Rockies in 2010 versus the Atlanta Braves.

MARTY CORDOVA
Left Field, Baltimore

What: Not a good place for a cat nap

Where: Baltimore

When: 5/22/2002

Story: The following is an absolute classic. Turns out that Marty wanted to get a tan and a nap. Well, you can't have both! He must have needed a nap because when Cordova awakened from his slumber, he quickly found out that his face was burnt! Whoever thought that one needed Coppertone when going to a tanning booth! Doctors told Cordova he should stay out of the sun as much as possible while the burn healed, so he had to miss a few games— day games that is!

MLB Debut: 4/26/95

Last MLB appearance: 4/21/03

Teams played for: Minnesota, Toronto, Cleveland, Baltimore

Career Stats: .274, 122 HR, 540 RBI

MARK SMITH
Outfield, Baltimore

What: Is working on equipment in your contract?

Where: Local hotel

When: 1994-1996

Story: The old saying that curiosity killed the cat almost cost Mark his hand. Mark was curious as to why the air conditioner wasn't working, so he stuck his hand in there to investigate, only to injure his hand. This act caused him to miss a few games.

MLB Debut: 5/14/94

Last MLB appearance: 9/28/03

Career Stats: .243, 32 HR, 138 RBI

Teams played for: Baltimore, Pittsburgh, Florida, Montreal, and Milwaukee

Fun Fact: On 7/12/97, hit a 3-run home run in the bottom of the 10th inning in a 0-0 game to give Pittsburgh a 3-0 win over the Houston Astros. The home run also ended the first extra-innings combined no-hitter in MLB history.

JIM CORSI
Pitcher, Baltimore

What: Where are my contacts?

Where: His house

When: 1999

Story: Corsi slipped coming out of the shower and sprained his wrist. Corsi had bad eyesight, wasn't wearing contacts, and misjudged the step. Gee, that's an understatement!

MLB debut: 6/28/88

Last MLB appearance: 10/3/99

Career Stats: 22-24, 3.25 ERA, 290 K

Teams played for: Oakland, Houston, Oakland, Florida, Oakland, Boston, Baltimore

DENNIS MARTINEZ
Pitcher, Baltimore

What: Carry-on bag that was too much to handle

Where: Baltimore

Story: Martinez chucked his luggage onto the team bus, and in the process injured his arm. The inside joke was that he was diagnosed with "Samsonitis."

MLB Debut: 9/14/76

Last MLB appearance: 9/27/98

Career Stats: 245-193, 3.70 ERA, 2,149 K

Teams played for: Baltimore, Montreal, Cleveland, Seattle, Atlanta

Accolades: 4 times All-Star, World Series champion (1983), MLB wins leader (1981), MLB ERA leader (1991)

Fun Fact: He was the first player from Nicaragua to play in the majors.

Fun Fact #2: Pitched a perfect game on 7/28/91, the first in Montreal Expos history.

Fun Fact #3: Became the first visiting pitcher to throw a no-hitter at Dodger Stadium.

Fun Fact #4: Ron Hassey was the catcher for Martinez's perfect game and was also the catcher for Len Barker's perfect game on 5/15/81, becoming the only catcher in major league history to catch multiple perfect games.

Fun Fact #5: One of nine players to win at least 100 wins in both the American and National League.

Fun Fact #6: Opening Day starter for Cleveland on 4/4/94, which was the first game in Jacobs Field; Tribe won 4-3 in 11 innings.

Fun Fact #7: Has the most career victories of any hurdler who has never won 20 games in a single season.

Houston Astros

HUNTER PENCE
Right Field, Houston

What: Glass door 1, Hunter 0

Where: Pence casa

When: 2/18/08

MLB Debut: 4/28/07

Story: Remember the scene in The Whole Nine Yards where Oz runs into the glass door while it's still closed? Pence did his impression of this but took it to another level and actually fell through a glass door he failed to realize was closed. He cut his hands and knees in the process. Can see it now as he might be quite skittish going to a glass door that is closed and touching the door before opening it.

Teams played for: Houston, Philadelphia, San Francisco, and Texas

Career Stats: .280, 1,786 H, 242 HR, 936 RBI, 120 SB

Accolades: 3 times All-Star, 2 times World Series Champion

MOISES ALOU
Outfield, Houston, Part I and II

What: The treadmill that bites back and the bike with no horn

Where: Alou house

When: 1998

Story: You would think that a stationary object such as a treadmill would be a safe exercise choice. Not at the Alou house.

Running on a treadmill at his house in the Dominican Republic before Spring Training started, Alou lost his footing and fell off—tearing the ACL in his left knee. If that wasn't enough, Alou worked his tail off to get back to the Astros late in the season—only to reinjure himself while riding a bicycle when he ran over his son. Guess when Moises looks at a bike nowadays, it better come with a horn! My question in all of this is: Did his son get a whopping from this?

MLB Debut: 7/26/90

Last MLB appearance: 6/10/08

Teams played for: Pittsburgh, Montreal, Florida, Houston, Chicago Cubs, San Francisco, New York Mets

Career Stats: .303, 332 HR, 1,287 RBI, 2,134 H

Accolades: 6 times All-Star, World Series Champion (1997), 2 times Silver Slugger Award

Fun Fact: Did not wear batting gloves but instead urinated on his hands to toughen them up.

Fun Fact #2: In 2008, he was one of four current major leaguers to hit 20 home runs in a season whose fathers had also hit 20 home runs in a season.

NOLAN RYAN
Pitcher, Houston

What: Wily Coyote

Where: Alvin, Texas

When: 1985

Story: Ryan went out to his dog pen to tend to them, only to be greeted by two coyote pups. He took the pups home with him, only to have one bite him on his pitching hand. Ryan had several tests done to make sure he did not have rabies. He ended up missing a start and giving the pups away.

Don't mess with Texas!

MLB Debut: 9/11/66

Last MLB appearance: 9/22/93

Career Stats: 324-292, 3.19 ERA, 5,714 K

Teams played for: New York Mets, California, Houston, Texas

Accolades: World Series champion (1969), 8 times All-Star, 2 times NL ERA leader, 11 times strikeout leader, major league records of 5,714 strikeouts and 7 no-hitters.

First-ballot Hall of Famer–1999.

Fun Fact: All-time major league holder in walks with 2,795.

Fun Fact #2: Batters hit .204 against Ryan, also a major league record.

Fun Fact #3: One of five pitchers in major league history to have more strikeouts than innings pitched.

Fun Fact #4: One of three players in major league history to have his number retired by three teams (California, Houston, and Texas)

Fun Fact #5: Along with his major league record of seven no-hitters, also has 12 one-hitters (tied with Bob Feller for the record), 18 two-hitters, and 31 three-hitters.

Fun Fact #6: Gave up his first major league home run to Joe Torre, a future National League and World Series champion manager.

Fun Fact #7: Only pitcher to strike out three batters on nine pitches in both the National and American League.

Fun Fact #8: Became the only player to play for all four MLB original expansion teams: New York Mets, California Angels, Houston Colt .45s/Astros and Washington Senators/Texas Rangers.

Fun Fact #9: His final pitch at the age of 46 was clocked at 98 miles per hour.

Fun Fact #10: Played in more seasons, 27, than any other player in major league history.

Fun Fact #11: Ryan struck out 7 different father/son combinations. That's something to be proud of if you were one of the lucky seven!

GEOFF BLUM
Infield, Houston

What: Cotton or polyester?

Where: Clubhouse

When: July 2010

Story: Who would have thought putting on a shirt after a game would cause you to miss the rest of the season? That is what happened to Geoff when he injured his elbow while putting on his shirt.

MLB Debut: 8/9/99

Last MLB appearance: 7/17/12

Career Stats: .250, 99 HR, 479 RBI

Teams played for: Montreal, Houston, Tampa Bay, San Diego, Chicago White Sox, San Diego, Houston, Arizona

Accolades: World Series champion (2005)

Texas Rangers

MARTIN PEREZ

Pitcher, Texas

What: Door's revenge

Where: New York

When: 6/24/17

Story: Well, there is nothing like after a long day at the ballpark and returning to your hotel room, only to have your tip of your right thumb fractured and the nail torn off as it is caught on the hinge of your door! Ouch! Guess he did not realize that doors in the U.S. close a whole lot faster than in Venezuela.

Perez is a lefty.

MLB Debut: 6/27/12

Teams played for: Texas and Minnesota

Career Stats: 53-56, 4.72 ERA, 597 K

JAKE DIEKMAN

Pitcher, Texas

What: Fragile but will travel

Where: Boston

When: July 2016

Story: On a road trip to Boston, Diekman picked up a souvenir mug from Cheers. The only problem was that it was packed a little too loosely, causing it to break and having a piece of glass cut his index finger.

Diekman is a lefty.

MLB Debut: 5/15/12

Teams played for: Philadelphia, Texas, Arizona, Kansas City, and Oakland

Career Stats: 15-22, 3.90 ERA, 467 K

Fun Fact: Pitched a combined no-hitter on 9/1/14

GREG HARRIS
Pitcher, Texas

What: Flick flick flicking away

Where: Texas

When: 1987

Story: Flicking sunflower seeds versus spitting them out. Greg chose the former.

Harris could pitch with both arms. Unfortunately, he could not flick with both hands. Because if he could, maybe he wouldn't have had to skip two starts after this incident during the 1987 season when he spent an entire game harassing his teammates with sunflower seeds. Can you imagine the looks on his teammates' faces when they found out he was missing two games because of that! Guess they had the last laugh.

A natural right-hander, by the 1986 season Harris could throw well enough left-handed that he felt he could pitch with either hand in a game, but the teams he played for would not allow this keeping him from being a legitimate ambidextrous major league pitcher. Harris wasn't allowed to throw lefty in a regular season game until September 28, 1995, his penultimate game with the Expos. In the ninth inning, Harris retired Reggie Sanders pitching right-handed, then switched to his left hand for the next two hitters, Hal Morris and Ed Taubensee, who both batted lefty. Harris walked Morris but got Taubensee to ground out. He then went back to his right hand to retire Bret Boone to end the inning. Harris' glove, which was custom built with an extra thumb so that it could be worn on either hand, is now on display at the Baseball Hall of Fame in Cooperstown, New York.

MLB Debut: 5/21/81

Last MLB Appearance: 9/29/95

Teams played for: New York Mets, Cincinnati, Montreal, San Diego, Texas, Philadelphia, Boston, New York Yankees, Montreal

Career Stats: 74-90, 3.69 ERA, 1,141 K

ELVIS ANDRUS
Shortstop, Texas

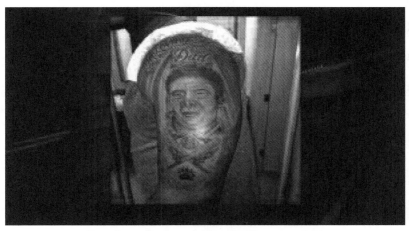

Sure hope they spelled my dad's name right.

What: The ink that keeps on giving

Where: 2/28/13

When: Spring Training

Story: Andrus spent 9 hours under the needle earlier in the week while getting a large tattoo of his late father on his left shoulder. After being under the needle for 9 hours—that's right, 9 hours!—he experienced a soreness. Gee, there's an understatement. The soreness caused him to miss a game, albeit an exhibition game.

MLB Debut: 4/6/09

Teams played for: Texas

Career Stats: .275, 73 HR, 1,723 H, 629 RBI, 302 SB

Accolades: 2 times All-Star

ODDIBE MCDOWELL
Center Field, Texas

What: Cuttin' biscuits turned out to be dangerous

Where: Texas clubhouse

When: 1987

Story: You've heard the phrase, "Cuts like a hot knife through butter." Oddibe did not subscribe to that theory. After getting home from an unsuccessful road trip to start the season, ownership threw together a spread. As Oddibe went to put butter on the biscuit per se, he ended up cutting his middle finger, requiring 8 stiches to close. Hope you enjoyed the biscuit, Oddibe!

MLB Debut: 5/19/85

Last MLB appearance: 8/10/94

Teams played for: Texas, Cleveland, Atlanta, Texas

Career Stats: .253, 74 HR, 266 RBI

Fun Fact: McDowell was the first player to hit for the cycle for the Rangers on 7/23/85.

CHARLIE HOUGH
Pitcher, Texas

What: Broken pinkie

Where: Unknown location

When: 1986

Story: At a party in early 1986, Charlie and one of his teammates shook hands and continued by locking fingers and shaking hands with their pinkies, resulting in a broken finger for Hough. Maybe that is where the fist-pump came about!

MLB Debut: 8/12/70

Last MLB appearance: 7/26/94

Career Stats: 216-216, 3.75 ERA, 2,362 K

Teams played for: Los Angeles, Texas, Chicago White Sox, Florida

Accolades: All-Star (1986)

Fun Fact: Hough was one of the hurlers who gave up one of the three home runs that Reggie Jackson of the Yankees hit on three straight pitches in Game 6 of the 1977 World Series.

Fun Fact #2: Led the league in complete games in 1984 with 17.

Fun Fact #3: His last complete game of that 1984 season, on 9/30, was unlucky, as Mike Witt of the California Angels threw a perfect game.

Fun Fact #4: At age 43, during parts of the 1991-1992 season, he pitched for the Chicago White Sox. His catcher was 43-year-old Carlton Fisk.

Fun Fact #5: Started the first game in Florida Marlins history in 1993, striking out the first batter (which was way outside by the way!).

Fun Fact #6: On 6/14/94, against St. Louis, became the oldest pitcher to pitch a shutout.

Fun Fact #7: Upon his retirement, at 46, he was the last active player to have been born in the 1940s.

JEFF BAKER
Utility Positions, Texas

What: Couldn't we have done a fist-pump?

Where: Arlington

When: 6/14/13

Story: Baker sprained his thumb upon giving a teammate an over-exuberant high five and bent his thumb back to the wrist. Ouch! That landed him on the disabled list for a month.

MLB Debut: 4/4/05

Last MLB appearance: 7/7/15

Career Stats: .264, 54 HR, 235 RBI

Teams played for: Colorado, Chicago Cubs, Detroit, Atlanta, Texas, Miami

DEREK HOLLAND

Pitcher, Texas

What: Get out of the way, Wrigley

Where: Holland house

When: January 2014

Story: At home during the off-season, Holland was playing with his boxer named Wrigley. As he was running upstairs, the dog tripped Holland, which caused him to make his first appearance after the All-Star break from knee surgery. So much for man's best friend!

Holland is a lefty.

MLB Debut: 4/25/09

Career Stats: 78-78, 4.54 ERA, 1,145 K

Teams played for: Texas, Chicago White Sox, San Francisco, Chicago Cubs, Pittsburgh

RICK HONEYCUTT

Pitcher, Texas

What: Watch what you wipe with

Where: Kansas City

When: 9/30/80

Story: Honeycutt was given the boot by the home plate umpire against the Royals for having a thumbtack taped to his pitching hand; he was suspended 10 games for this incident. What makes this funnier is that he suffered a deep scratch on his forehead for wiping his brow with the thumbtack still on his hand!

Honeycutt is a lefty.

MLB Debut: 8/24/77

Last MLB appearance: 5/2/97

Career Stats: 109-143, 3.72 ERA, 1,038 K

Teams played for: Seattle, Texas, Los Angeles, Oakland, Texas, Oakland, New York Yankees, St. Louis

Accolades: 2 times All-Star, World Series champion (1989), AL ERA leader (1983)

Fun Fact: Having pitched in 30 post-season games, he went undefeated, going 3-0.

Seattle Mariners

RUSSELL BRANYON
First Baseman, Seattle

What: Going out to eat gets physical

Where: Pizza parlor

When: September 2010

Story: It was pizza night for the Branyon clan. They were seated on plastic chairs. Branyon's son dropped something on the floor. As Branyon went to pick it up, the plastic chair slid out from under him and Branyon landed on his tailbone. Russell missed 5 games.

Guess he was trying to beat the 5-second rule!

In addition to the above injury, Branyon also missed 4 games while with the Mariners. While closing the curtains in a hotel, he cut his toe on the table.

MLB Debut: 9/26/98

Last MLB appearance: 9/26/11

Teams played for: Cleveland, Cincinnati, Milwaukee, Tampa Bay, San Diego, Philadelphia, St. Louis, Milwaukee, Seattle, Cleveland, Seattle, Arizona, Los Angeles Angels.

Career Stats: .232, 194 HR, 467 RBI

Fun Fact: Only player to date to hit a home run into the 4th deck of the new Yankee Stadium

Fun Fact #2: Branyan was arrested for breaking into his ex-wife's home in Tennessee while she was asleep. Branyan removed several items from the home and adjusted the thermostat to a very cold temperature. I'm not advocating breaking into a home, but to turn down the thermostat is classic!!

KEN GRIFFEY JR.

Center Field, Seattle

What: Cup and testicle

Where: In the field

When: 1990s

Story: Apparently, Griffey's cup and testicle did not fit well together as the former pinched the latter, resulting in an injury that caused him to miss a game. Imagine the equipment kid getting an earful from Junior.

MLB Debut: 4/3/89

Last MLB appearance: 5/31/10

Teams played for: Seattle, Cincinnati, Chicago White Sox, Seattle

Career Stats: .284, 630 HR, 1,836 RBI, 2,781 H

Accolades: 13 times All-Star, AL MVP (1987), 10 times Gold Glover, 7 times Silver Slugger, NL Comeback Player of the Year (2005), 4 times AL home run leader, AL RBI leader (1997)

First-ballot Hall of Famer–2016

Fun Fact: His first major league hit was a double.

Fun Fact #2: Played two seasons with his dad (1990 and 1991) becoming the first father and son to play on the same team at the same time. Also, both senior and junior hit back-to-back home runs, becoming the first father and son to do so.

REY QUINONES
Shortstop, Seattle

Where: Seattle clubhouse

What: Rey you're up…Rey…Rey…anyone see Rey?

When: 1987

Story: Rey was called on to pinch hit in a game, only to miss that opportunity because he was back in the clubhouse playing Nintendo. Guess getting to the 7th level of Super Mario Brothers is more important than doing your job!

MLB Debut: 5/17/86

Last MLB appearance: 7/21/89

Career Stats: .243, 29 HR, 159 RBI

Teams played for: Boston, Seattle, Pittsburgh

Fun Fact: Received a World Series ring from the 1996 New York Yankees but was later sold at auction. Perhaps Rey needed cash to get the new gaming system.

Anaheim Angels

ALLEN WATSON

Pitcher, Anaheim Angels

What: Twist top is better

Where: Parts unknown

When: 1998 season

Story: Angel's pitcher Allen Watson cut the wrist on his pitching arm while trying to open a bottle of beer.

We're not sure how many beers Watson had before the incident, but I'm guessing he had a few.

***Funny story: There was an incident where Watson was horsing around in the Yankee clubhouse and threw a bagel toward a clubhouse attendant, just as Yankee owner George Steinbrenner walked in. When the bagel hit Steinbrenner, he demanded to know who threw it. When Watson confessed, Steinbrenner remarked, "I figured it was you, Watson. That's why it didn't hurt."

Watson is a lefty.

MLB Debut: 7/8/93

Last MLB appearance: 8/10/00

Teams played for: St. Louis, San Francisco, Anaheim, New York Mets, Seattle, New York Yankees

Accolades: World Series Champion (1999-2000)

Career Stats: 51-55, 5.03 ERA, 589 K

CHRIS BOOTCHECK

Pitcher, Anaheim

What: Stretch before running to break up brawl!

Where: Anaheim Stadium

When: 5/2/06

Story: Bootcheck was anxious to jump into the John Lackey/Jason Kendall brouhaha but strained his hamstring running in from the bullpen. He landed on the 15-day disabled list but ended up missing the rest of the season. Sure hoping he got a few shots in!

MLB Debut: 9/9/03

Last MLB appearance: 6/14/13

Career Stats: 3-7, 6.55 ERA, 106 K

Teams played for: Anaheim, Pittsburgh, New York Yankees

GARY DiSARCINA
Shortstop, Anaheim Angels

What: Know your surroundings

Where: Tempe, AZ

When: February 1999

Story: This is not a good way to start your season: Two days before the Angels first team workout, DiSarcina walked out of the batting cage into a fungo bat used by first-base coach George Hendricks who was hitting grounders to the infielders. This broke DiSarcina's left forearm and caused him to miss the first two months of the season.

MLB Debut: 9/23/89

Last MLB appearance: 5/8/00

Career Stats: .258, 28 HR, 355 RBI

Teams played for: California/Anaheim

Accolades: All-Star (1995)

Fun Fact: Made the last out in Kenny Rogers' perfect game on 7/28/94.

MO VAUGHN
First Base, Anaheim

What: Bombs away

Where: Anaheim

When: 2000 season

Story: Vaughn's start to his Anaheim career did not begin well in 1999, as he fell down the visitors' dugout steps on the first play of his first game. In 2000, he ended up missing a game when a piece of drywall from a leaking ceiling tile fell and landed on his eye, causing him to miss a game.

MLB Debut: 6/27/91

Last MLB appearance: 5/2/03

Career Stats: .293, 328 HR, 1,064 RBI

Teams played for: Boston, Anaheim, New York Mets

Accolades: 3 times All-Star, AL MVP (1995), Silver Slugger and AL RBI Leader (1995)

KENDRYS MORALES
Designated Hitter and First Base, Los Angeles Angels

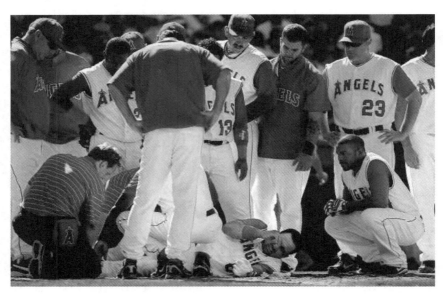

What: Celebration gone astray

Where: Anaheim, California

When: 5/29/10

Story: Who thought that running around the bases could be hazardous for your health. As the old saying goes, from the thrill of victory to the agony of defeat. From hitting a grand slam to win a game to being on the disabled list for over a year and a half—this is how Morales made this list.

After hitting a game-winning grand slam off of Mariners' closer Brandon League in the bottom of the 10th inning, Morales jumped up as he reached his team surrounding home plate.

As soon as he landed, he continued on his way down to the ground, suffering a broken leg in the celebration. The injury would cost Morales all but 51 games of the 2010 season and the entire 2011 campaign.

MLB Debut: 5/23/06

Teams played for: Los Angeles Angels of Anaheim, Seattle, Minnesota, Seattle, Kansas City, Toronto, Oakland, New York Yankees

Career Stats: .265, 213 HR, 1,289 H, 740 RBI

World Series Champion (2015)

Accolades: Silver Slugger Award (2015)

Fun Fact: On 7/30/12 hit two home runs in the same inning as a switch hitter. He became only the third player in history to accomplish that feat in the same inning.

JIM BARR
Pitcher, California Angels

What: Watch what you hit

Where: Anaheim

When: September 1979

Story: Barr helped the Angels reach the playoffs for the first time in their franchise history in 1979, but was unable to pitch in the series because of a broken right hand. Apparently, a fan held up a sign that had a toilet seat that said the "Angels are #2." Jim didn't realize that the seat was an actual toilet seat, took a swipe at it and broke his hand, knocking him out of the playoffs.

MLB debut: 7/31/71

Last MLB appearance: 10/2/83

Career Stats: 101-112, 3.56 ERA, 741 K

Teams played for: San Francisco, California

Fun Fact: Holds the record for consecutive batters retired (41) over two games.

BOBBY GRICH

Second Baseman, California

What: Call a mover

Where: His house

When: Spring 1977

Story: Grich was a little too eager to move an air conditioner, because he ended up with a herniated lumbar disk in his back, which caused him to miss most of the 1977 season with the California Angels. He had signed with the Angels after spending the first seven years of his career with Baltimore.

MLB Debut: 6/29/70

Last MLB appearance: 10/2/86

Career Stats: .266, 224 HR, 864 RBI

Teams played for: Baltimore and California

Accolades: 6 times All-Star, 4 times Gold Glove Award, Silver Slugger Award (1981), AL home run leader (1981), World Series champion (1970).

Fun Fact: In 1981, became the first second baseman in the American League to lead the league in home runs, since 1901.

Fun Fact #2: During the media interview after the Game 7 loss to the Red Sox in the 1986 ALCS, he announced his retirement.

Oakland Athletics

DREW POMERANZ
Pitcher, Oakland

What: Temper temper!

Where: Oakland

When: June 2014

Story: Pomeranz broke his right hand when he punched a chair after getting hit around by the Rangers. That temper tantrum cost him 15 days on the disabled list with a fractured right hand.

Pomeranz is a lefty.

MLB Debut: 9/11/11

Teams played for: Colorado, Oakland, San Diego, Boston, San Francisco, Milwaukee, San Diego

Career Stats: 46-58, 4.04 ERA, 824 K

Accolades: World Series Champion 2018

RICH HARDEN
Pitcher, Oakland

What: No snoozing allowed!

Where: Harden house

When: 2004

Story: Raise your hand if you look forward to turning off the alarm clock or better yet y'all have heard, "Man, he woke up on the wrong side of the bed." Harden takes it to another level with this story. Seems he strained his shoulder as he went to turn off the alarm clock. Hey man, put that noise maker on the other side of the room so you have to get up and walk over to turn it off!

MLB appearance: 7/21/03

Last MLB appearance: 9/25/11

Teams played for: Oakland, Chicago Cubs, Texas, Oakland

Career Stats: 59-38, 3.76 ERA, 949 K

Fun Fact: Became the 38th pitcher to strike out three batters on nine pitches, which he accomplished on 6/8/08.

MICHAEL TAYLOR
Outfielder, Oakland

What: Underhand toss would work better

Where: Spring Training, Mesa, Arizona

When: March 2013

Story: Now when you are 6'5", you would think that from experience you would know how tall the ceilings are. Well, Taylor seemed to forget that as he tried to throw away a piece of sticky bubblegum. It seemed that sticky sucker did not want to let go of his hand. As he flung his hand overhand, he hit a light on the dugout ceiling which opened a nasty gash on his right pinkie-finger. At that point, he'd already been out a week and was told that he couldn't return to action until the cut had fully healed.

MLB Debut: 9/2/11

Last MLB appearance: 9/28/14

Career Stats: .167, 1 HR, 1 RBI

Teams played for: Oakland and Chicago White Sox

New York Mets

BOB OJEDA

Pitcher, New York Mets

What: The "honey-do" list that went astray

Where: Ojeda house

When: 9/22/88

Story: Next time Bob is asked to do some honey do's around the house, don't blame the guy if he breaks out into cold sweats. After reading this story, who could blame him! The honeysuckle bushes needed trimming at the Ojeda casa on a cool fall day, leading up to the playoffs I might add, kind of one of the most important parts of the year for his team, the Mets. As he was going about trimming them up, the electric hedge clipper nearly severed the upper part of his left middle finger. He needed microsurgery to reattach the fingertip. He ended up missing the post-season for the Mets who lost to the Dodgers in the NLCS.

Ojeda is a lefty.

MLB Debut: 7/13/80

Last MLB appearance: 4/22/94

Teams played for: Boston, New York Mets, Los Angeles Dodgers, Cleveland, New York Yankees

Career Stats: 115-98, 3.65 ERA, 1,128 K

World Series Champion (1986)

Fun Fact: On 6/23/81, was the winning pitcher in the longest professional baseball game in history, 33 innings between Pawtucket Red Sox and the Rochester Red Wings. Ironically, Wade Boggs and Cal Ripken Jr. played in the game as well.

DWIGHT GOODEN
Pitcher, New York Mets

What: Fore!

Where: Mets clubhouse

When: 1993 season

Story: Seems Vince Coleman was working on his golf swing when Gooden's shoulder got in the way with his 9-Iron. Wasn't sure if that was on the up-swing or the down-swing, but either way Gooden missed a game because of that. Surely Coleman gave Gooden an extra mulligan the next time they played golf.

MLB Debut: 4/7/84

Last MLB appearance: 9/29/00

Career Stats: 194-112. 3.51 ERA, 2,293 K

Teams played for: New York Mets, New York Yankees, Cleveland, Houston, Tampa Bay, New York Yankees

Accolades: NL Rookie of the Year (1984), 4 times All-Star, 3 times World Series champion, NL Cy Young (1985), 2 times MLB strikeout leader.

Fun Fact: Became the youngest person to appear in an All-Star Game at the age of 19.

Fun Fact #2: As a rookie, in 1984, led the NL in strikeouts, with 276, breaking Cleveland's Herb Score's record of 245 in 1955.

Fun Fact #3: On 7/15/86, became the youngest pitcher to start an All-Star game at the age of 21.

Fun Fact #4: Pitched a no-hitter on 5/14/96, the first one by a Yankee right-hand pitcher since Don Larson's perfect game in the 1956 World Series.

TOM GLAVINE

Pitcher, New York Mets Story #1

What: Road rage in the Big Apple

Where: New York

When: August 2004

Story: Glavine lost two teeth and needed 40-45 stiches on his chin after a taxi ride accident. The crazy thing about this episode is that it took eight months for his mouth to heal before he got his permanent replacement teeth. Bet Tom is happy that Uber came along.

Atlanta Braves

TOM GLAVINE

Pitcher, Atlanta Story #2

What: No seconds for me, thank you

Where: Airplane flight

When: 1992

Story: On a flight home, Glavine ate something that did not agree with his stomach, so much so that he broke a rib upchucking the contents! Glavine did not miss a start because of a pain-killer shot.

Glavine is a lefty.

MLB Debut: 8/17/87

Last MLB appearance: 8/14/08

Career Stats: 305-203, 3.54 ERA, 2,607 K

Teams played for: Atlanta, New York Mets, Atlanta

First-ballot Hall of Famer–2014

Accolades: 10 times All-Star, World Series champion and MVP (1995), 2 times NL Cy Young Award, 4 times Silver Slugger Award, 5 times NL wins leader

Fun Fact: Was drafted by the NHL's Los Angeles Kings in the 1984 draft.

Fun Fact #2: Won 20 games for three straight years from 1991-1993; he was the last pitcher to do that.

Fun Fact #3: 6/27/07, Glavine for the Mets, and former teammates (Greg Maddux for the Padres and John Smoltz for the Braves) all recorded wins.

Fun Fact #4: One of only six left-handers to have over 300 career wins.

RYAN KLESKO
Left Field, First Base, Atlanta

What: No seconds for you, Ryan!

Where: Clubhouse

Story: Seems that whatever they were serving at the lunchroom that Klesko wasn't shy about seconds. He ended up hyperextending his back when he picked the tray up and attempted to return the tray.

MLB Debut: 9/12/92

Last MLB appearance: 9/29/07

Career Stats: .279, 278 HR, 987 RBI

Team played for: Atlanta, San Diego, San Francisco

Accolades: All-Star (2001), World Series champion (1995)

Fun Fact: Hit a home run in three consecutive World Series games in 1995.

Fun Fact #2: In Game 5 of the 1995 World Series, his home run was almost caught by his mom. Klesko traded an autographed Greg Maddux baseball in exchange for that ball.

RON GANT
Outfield, Atlanta

What: Aaron Boone, part 2

Where: His property

When: 1994

Story: Shortly after signing the richest contract in Atlanta Braves history, Gant went out for a motorcycle ride but ended up breaking his right leg. Like the Yankees did to Boone, the Braves released Gant and he did not play until the '95 season.

MLB Debut: 9/6/87

Last MLB appearance: 5/25/03

Career Stats: .256, 321 HR, 1,008 RBI

Teams played for: Atlanta, Cincinnati, St. Louis, Philadelphia, Anaheim, Colorado, Oakland, San Diego

Accolades: 2 times All-Star, Silver Slugger Award (1991)

CECIL UPSHAW
Pitcher, Atlanta

What: He won the bet but lost his career

Where: San Diego

When: Spring 1970

Story: Upshaw and two of his teammates were walking down the sidewalk one particular day when one of them bet that Upshaw could not jump up and touch an awning. Cecil touched the awning, but a ring on his pitching hand got caught on the awning and tore ligaments in his hand. He never fully recovered.

MLB Debut: 10/1/66

Last MLB appearance: 9/28/75

Career Stats: 34-36, 3.13 ERA, 323 K, 86 SV

Teams played for: Atlanta, Houston, Cleveland, New York Yankees

ERICK AYBAR
Shortstop, Atlanta

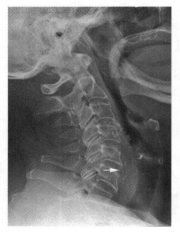

That X-ray says it all!

What: Bone-in versus boneless

Where: His home

When: 5/19/16

Story: The shortstop was removed from the starting lineup for a game against the Pittsburgh Pirates after a chicken bone got stuck in his throat. He was taken to the doctor and had the bone removed.

How about sitting down with the family for some chicken wings when next thing you know, Erick can't breathe too well. Needless to say, he'll be getting boneless wings from now on!

MLB Debut: 5/16/06

Teams played for: Los Angeles Angels, Atlanta, Detroit, San Diego, and Minnesota

Career Stats: .271, 58 HR, 473 RBI, 1,402 H, 155 SB

Accolades: All-Star (2014), Gold Glove Award (2011)

PASCUAL PEREZ
Pitcher, Atlanta

What: Ask for directions

Where: Atlanta

When: 8/19/1982

Story: Perez just received his license and while driving to Atlanta-Fulton County Stadium, he ended up circling Atlanta's beltway 3 times. After two hours, he ran out of gas and arrived at the ballpark ten minutes late, missing his start. After this incident he earned the nickname "Wrong-Way Perez."

MLB Debut: 5/7/80

Last MLB appearance: 10/2/91

Career Stats: 67-68, 3.44 ERA, 822 K

Teams played for: Pittsburgh, Atlanta, Montreal, New York Yankees

Accolades: All-Star (1983)

TERRY HARPER
Outfield, Atlanta

What: Leave the sign waving to the coaches

Where: Atlanta

When: 1985

Story: In his over exuberance, Harper injured his shoulder, waving another runner home and high fiving him.

MLB Debut: 9/12/80

Last MLB appearance: 10/2/87

Career Stats: .253, 36 HR, 180 RBI

Teams played for: Atlanta, Detroit, Pittsburgh

Washington Nationals

JOEY EISCHEN
Pitcher, Washington

What: Go for broke dive

Where: Washington

When: May 2005

Story: This just hurts when you read it: Eischen was injured when he fell to the ground and landed on his glove hand after fielding a ground ball. He told reporters that he heard a "snap" when he landed. Ouch! Needless to say, he went on the disabled list for over two months.

Eischen is a lefty.

MLB Debut: 6/19/94

Last MLB appearance: 5/29/06

Career Stats: 11-9, 3.67 ERA, 244 K

Teams played for: Montreal, Los Angeles Dodgers, Detroit, Cincinnati, Montreal/Washington

Fun Fact: Eischen had to wear a mouth guard, as he would grind his teeth when pitching.

MARK DEROSA
Utility Positons, Washington

What: Know why you went on the disabled list

Where: Washington

When: 5/7/12

Story: DeRosa was on the disabled list with a left oblique strain. During a game against Philadelphia, Bryce Harper stole home, and Mark gave him a celebratory high five with his left hand, further injuring the left side of his oblique.

MLB Debut: 9/2/98

Last MLB appearance: 9/29/13

Career Stats: .268, 100 HR, 494 RBI

Teams played for: Atlanta, Texas, Chicago Cubs, Cleveland, St. Louis, San Francisco, Washington, Toronto

Montreal Expos

Carlos Perez   157

CARLOS PEREZ

Pitcher, Montreal

What: Self-inflicted broken nose

Where: Montreal

When: July 1998

Story: Apparently, he lost control of the car and struck a lamp post near Olympic Stadium as he was trying to pass the team bus! The result of this was a broken nose.

Perez is a lefty.

MLB Debut: 4/27/95

Last MLB appearance: 9/5/00

Career Stats: 40-53, 4.44 ERA, 448 K

Teams played for: Montreal and Los Angeles

Accolades: All-Star (1995)

Philadelphia Phillies

DICK ALLEN
First Base, Third Base, Outfield, Philadelphia

What: Be careful where you place your hand!

Where: Philadelphia

When: 8/24/67

Story: Allen got out of his stalled car to push it up a driveway. Then he put his hand through the glass covering the headlight, cutting his hand badly enough to sever a tendon. Because of the injury, Allen missed the rest of the season and would have little sensation in the two middle fingers on his throwing hand.

MLB Debut: 9/3/63

Last MLB appearance: 6/19/77

Career Stats: .292, 351 HR, 1,119 RBI

Teams played for: Philadelphia, St. Louis, Los Angeles Dodgers, Chicago White Sox, Philadelphia, Oakland

Accolades: NL Rookie of the Year (1964), 7 times All-Star, AL MVP (1972), 2 times AL home run leader, AL RBI leader (1972)

Fun Fact: Had two brothers that also played in the majors.

Fun Fact #2: On 5/29/65, hit a two-run home run that cleared the Coke sign on the roof of Connie Mack Stadium which is 65 feet high. That home run was an estimated 529-footer, one of the longest measured in baseball history.

Fun Fact #3: 7/31/72, Allen became the first player to hit two inside-the-park home runs in one game. Both homers were hit off Bert Blyleven.

Fun Fact #4: In his final at bat of his career, hit a single.

CURT SIMMONS
Pitcher, Philadelphia

What: Hire a kid to do the yard, Curt

Where: His house

When: 6/5/53

Story: Curt was taking care of one the honey-do's at the Simmons house when he cut off a part of his big toe while mowing the lawn. That placed him on the disabled list for a month.

Simmons is a lefty.

MLB Debut: 9/28/47

Last MLB appearance: 10/1/67

Career Stats: 193-193, 3.54 ERA, 1,697 K

Teams played for: Philadelphia, St. Louis, Chicago Cubs, California

Accolades: 3 times All-Star, World Series champion (1964)

Fun Fact: Both Hank Aaron and Stan Musial commented that Simmons was the toughest pitcher they ever faced.

JEFF JUDEN
Pitcher, Philadelphia

What: Don't sunbathe after a tattoo

Where: Spring Training

When: 1994

Story: Juden was fresh off getting a new tattoo when he failed to read the fine print of his tattoo agreement and went out to get a suntan. Unbeknownst to him, the interaction of the sun with the new tattoo caused an infection, which made him miss a start.

MLB Debut: 9/15/91

Last MLB appearance: 10/3/99

Career Stats: 27-32, 4.81 ERA, 441 K

Teams played for: Houston, Philadelphia, San Francisco, Montreal, Cleveland, Milwaukee, Anaheim, New York Yankees

Miami Marlins

BRET BARBERIE

Infield, Florida

What: Wash your hands, Bret

Where: Unknown location

When: May 1994

Story: Bret decided to make some himself some nachos, spicy nachos that is. He loaded some tortilla chips with spicy peppers covered in habanero chili sauce and went to town. Problem was, he forgot to wash his hands before putting his contact lenses in and scorched his retinas. Needless to say, he missed a game.

MLB Debut: 6/16/91

Last MLB appearance: 6/22/96

Teams played for: Montreal, Florida, Baltimore and Chicago Cubs

Career Stats: .271, 16 HR, 133 RBI

Fun Fact: He recorded the first hit in Marlins franchise history off Orel Hershiser.

CHRIS COGHLAN

Outfield, Florida Marlins

I sure hope I stick this landing!

What: The art of the surprise = a torn meniscus

Where: Miami, Florida

When: 7/25/10

Story: After the Marlins' Wes Helms

hit the game winning single against the Atlanta Braves in the bottom of the 10th inning in a game between these division rivals, Coghlan was understandably fired up! So much so that he chased Helms down, jumping over his back to smash the pie in his face. The problem was that he did not nail the landing, which resulted in tearing the meniscus in his left knee. He missed the rest of the year, but the sad part was that his career was never the same.

MLB Debut: 5/8/09

Teams played for: Florida/Miami Marlins, Chicago Cubs, Oakland, Chicago Cubs, Toronto

Career Stats: .258, 53 HR, 234 RBI

Accolades: NL Rookie of the Year (2009), World Series Champion (2016)

MARK BUEHRLE
Pitcher, Miami

What: All I wanted was a little mayo!

Where: Miami clubhouse

When: 4/12/12

Story: The pitcher sliced the thumb on his pitching hand a few hours before a game against the Phillies, while opening a jar of mayonnaise. While the injury did not force him to miss his start, Buehrle said it was on his mind in the first inning when he allowed a hit, walked a batter, and hit another.

Buehrle is a lefty.

MLB Debut: 7/16/00

Last MLB appearance: 10/4/15

Career Stats: 214-160, 3.81 ERA, 1,870 K

Teams played for: Chicago White Sox, Miami Marlins, Toronto

Accolades: 5 Times All-Star , World Series Champion (2005), 4 times Gold Glove winner.

Fun Fact: Pitched a no-hitter on 4/18/07 and on that no hitter, after walking Sammy Sosa, he then proceeded to pick him off first base.

Fun Fact #2: Pitched a perfect game on 7/23/09.

RANDY VERES
Pitcher, Florida

What: Quiet down over there

Where: Pittsburgh

When: 8/20/95

Story: Randy wasn't getting the rest that he needed at the hotel he was staying at because of the noise coming from the next room, so instead of going over there and talking to them personally, he proceeded to punch the headboard on his bed. His pitching hand, nonetheless, suffered a swollen tendon in his right pinkie and landed him on the disabled list.

MLB Debut: 7/1/89

Last MLB appearance: 6/23/97

Career Stats: 9-13, 4.60 ERA, 116 K

Teams played for: Milwaukee, Chicago Cubs, Florida, Detroit, Kansas City

Milwaukee Brewers

STEVE SPARKS

Pitcher, Milwaukee

What: Yellow pages or white pages

Where: Spring Training, Chandler, Arizona

When: 1994

Story: After sitting through a motivational seminar in spring training with the Brewers in 1994, reliever Steve Sparks was fired up. A group called "Radical Reality" had spoken to the club and part of their act was to have them rip phone books in half with their bare hands.

Full of energy, Sparks did what any excited player would do in order to get his teammates going—he reached for the nearest phone book and attempted to rip it in half, just like the musclemen.

Unfortunately for Sparks, he managed to dislocate his left shoulder. Said Brewers' trainer John Adam, "This is one of the freakiest injuries I've ever seen. And a bit annoying because I had to look up a phone number later."

MLB Debut: 4/28/95

Last MLB appearance: 9/26/04

Teams played for: Milwaukee, Anaheim Angels, Detroit, Oakland, Arizona

Career Stats: 59-76, 4.88 ERA, 658 K

WILL SMITH

Pitcher, Milwaukee

What: Full contact shower

Where: At the ballpark

When: Spring Training 2016

Story: Smith said he was getting ready to shower after pitching and was standing on one leg to take off his other shoe when he lost his balance and twisted his knee.

Well, we've all done this before, trying to take off our shoe by standing on one leg. Smith took this to another level as he was taking off his spikes. He fell and tore a ligament in his knee and was put on the disabled list.

Fun Fact: He was ejected on 5/21/15 for having a foreign substance on his arm.

MLB Debut: 5/23/12

Teams played for: Kansas City, Milwaukee and San Francisco

Career Stats: 20-22, 3.67 ERA, 398 K

Accolades: Willie Mac Award (2018) in honor of Giant great Willie McCovey

JONATHAN LUCROY
Catcher, Milwaukee

What: How am I going to explain this, honey?

Where: Unknown hotel

When: May 2012

Story: Brewers catcher Jonathan Lucroy was reaching under his hotel room bed for a lost sock when his wife shifted a suitcase, causing it to fall on his hand. Lucroy suffered a broken hand and required surgery. To make matters worse, his wife received hate mail on Facebook from irate fans. It should be noted that the Brewers were not exactly off to a hot start, getting out of the gates at 20-28.

MLB Debut: 5/21/10

Career Stats: .274, 108 HR, 545 RBI

Teams played for: Milwaukee, Texas, Colorado, Oakland, Los Angeles Angels, Chicago Cubs

Accolades: 2 times All-Star

Fun Fact: In 2012, became the first catcher to have two games in a single season with 7 or more RBIs.

RICHIE SEXSON
First Base, Milwaukee

What: If the hat doesn't fit, you must quit

Where: Spring Training

When: 2003

Story: Sexson missed the Brewers first intrasquad game with a strained neck, suffered while he was adjusting his cap during photo day. Too bad the Brewers did not have an adjustable cap.

MLB Debut: 9/14/97

Last MLB Appearance: 8/13/08

Teams played for: Cleveland, Milwaukee, Arizona, Seattle, New York Yankees

Career Stats: .261, 306 HR, 943 RBI

Accolades: 2 times All-Star

PAUL MOLITOR

Second Base Third Base, Designated Hitter, Milwaukee

What: Get out of the way, Brook!

Where: Cleveland

When: June 1990

Story: As Molitor hustled down the first base line, he bumped into Indians first baseman's Brook Jacoby and his finger got caught in Jacoby's glove. X-rays revealed a broken knuckle on his left index finger. He was placed on the disabled list for 4-6 weeks.

MLB Debut: 4/7/78

Last MLB appearance: 9/27/98

Career Stats: .306, 3,319 H, 234 HR, 1,307 RBI, 504 SB

Teams played for: Milwaukee, Toronto, Minnesota

Accolades: 7 times All-Star, World Series champion and MVP (1993), 4 times Silver Slugger Award

First-ballot Hall of Famer–2004; he was the first player inducted as a designated hitter.

Fun Fact: First player to have 5 hits in a World Series game; he accomplished this in Game 1 of the 1982 World Series.

Fun Fact #2: Had the 5th longest hitting streak in baseball history, with a 39 game hitting streak in 1987.

Fun Fact #3: First player to get his 3,000th hit on a triple.

Fun Fact #4: One of five players with at least 3,000 hits, a .300 lifetime batting average, and 500 stolen bases. Out of those five players, he is the only one with 200 home runs.

Fun Fact #5: Hit .300 across three decades.

DAVE NILSSON

Catcher, Milwaukee

What: Shoo fly, don't bother me!

Where: Australia

When: Winter 1994

Story: Nilsson missed the first two months of the '95 season after getting bit by a mosquito and contracting Ross River Fever. Ironically, this affects just 200 out of the 17 million residents in Australia. Don't believe that Nilsson felt like one of the lucky ones.

MLB Debut: 5/18/92

Last MLB appearance: 10/3/99

Career Stats: .284, 105 HR, 470 RBI

Teams played for: Milwaukee

Accolades: All-Star (1999)

Fun Fact: In 1999, Nilsson became the first Australian to appear in an All-Star game.

SCOOTER GENNETT
Second Baseman, Milwaukee

What: Pass the soap

Where: Pittsburgh

When: 4/19/15

Story: Who knew that reaching for soap would be so hazardous? Seems Gennett was reaching for the body wash in the shower, only to have his knuckle of his right index finger (his throwing hand) scrape against the metal corner of the soap holder. This required several stiches and a date on the 15-day disabled list. Bet he might try the soap on the rope next time!

MLB Debut: 6/3/13

Career Stats: .287, 87 HR, 360 RBI

Teams played for: Milwaukee, Cincinnati, San Francisco

Accolades: All-Star (2017)

Fun Fact: Became the 17th player in history to hit four home runs in a game, which he did on 6/6/17; was the 7th player to do that on four consecutive at bats; also became the first member of the Cincinnati Reds to accomplish that.

Fun Fact #2: 8/14/17, Scooter hit his 20th home run of the season and pitched one inning. Babe Ruth is the only other person to have hit his 20th home run and pitch in the same game.

St. Louis Cardinals

MATT HOLLIDAY
Left Field, St. Louis

What: Practice swings = missing games = who knew

Where: St. Louis

When: 9/15/11

Story: He missed four to five days with an injured right hand, hurt while taking practice swings in the on-deck circle. Guess his voracious swings caused an inflamed tendon in his middle finger.

   ***To be noted as well that on 8/22/11, Holliday had to leave a game because a moth flew into his ear. When I saw the video, my ears started to itch just looking at it!

Teams played for: Colorado, Oakland, St. Louis, New York Yankees, Colorado

MLB Debut: 4/16/04

Last MLB appearance: 10/7/18

Career Stats: .299, 316 HR, 1,220 RBI, 2,096 H

Accolades: 7 times All-Star, World Series Champion (2011), NLCS MVP (2011), 4 times Silver Slugger Award, NL Batting Champion (2007), NL RBI leader (2007)

VINCE COLEMAN
Left Field, St. Louis

What: The Tarp: It covereth, it taketh away!

Where: St. Louis

When: 10/13/85

Story: While the Cardinals were warming up for Game 4 of the NLCS against the Dodgers, a button was pushed to activate the Busch Stadium automated tarpaulin. Coleman did not see or hear the tarp that weighed over a half ton and was 180 feet in length (known as the killer tarp), coming toward him. It ended up rolling up behind him and catching his legs.

This knocked Coleman out of the rest of the playoffs, including the World Series, where the Cardinals lost to the Royals in seven games.

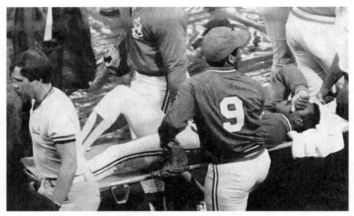

Come on guys, a little warning would have been nice!

MLB Debut: 4/18/85

Last MLB appearance: 4/14/97

Teams played for: St. Louis, New York Mets, Kansas City, Seattle, Cincinnati, Detroit

Career Stats: .264, 28 HR, 346 RBI, 752 SB

Accolades: 2 times All-Star, NL Rookie of the Year (1985), 6 times NL stolen base leader (1985-1990)

Fun Fact: Ranks 6th all-time in stolen bases; only player in history to have 3 consecutive seasons of 100 or more stolen bases in their first three seasons.

MARC RZEPCZYNSKI
Pitcher, St. Louis

What: Who knew golf is a full contact sport

Where: Viera, Florida

When: March 2013

MLB Debut: 7/7/09

Story: St. Louis Cardinals pitcher Marc Rzepczynski was injured at a golf outing during spring training when an acorn or a piece of debris flew up and hit the reliever around his left eye. Rzepczynski missed his scheduled start and was listed as day-to-day.

Rzepczynski is a lefty.

Teams played for: Toronto, St. Louis, Cleveland, San Diego, Oakland, Washington, Seattle, and Cleveland

Career Stats: 14-27, 3.89 ERA, 409 K

Accolades: World Series Champion (2011)

Fun Fact: Nickname is Scrabble

FLINT RHEM
Pitcher, St. Louis

What: Prohibition, yeah right!

Where: St. Louis

When: 1930

Story: Rhem went AWOL at the height of the 1930 pennant race. It wasn't his fault, he explained to Branch Rickey. Gamblers kidnapped him and forced him to drink whiskey for two days. While his manager, Gabby Street, couldn't disprove the accusation, he was put back into the rotation. Sixteen days after escaping the kidnappers, Rehm started Game 2 of the World Series.

MLB Debut: 9/6/24

Last MLB appearance: 8/26/36

Career Stats: 105-97, 4.20 ERA, 529 K

Teams played for: St. Louis, Philadelphia, Boston Braves

Accolades: 2 times World Series champion, NL wins leader (1926)

DANNY COX
Pitcher, St. Louis

What: Off day proved to be hazardous

Where: St. Petersburg, Florida

When: Spring Training 1986

Story: On an off day, Cox went fishing but ended up fracturing his right ankle jumping off a three-foot sea wall into the sand. Ironically, Cox was not supposed to make the road trip to Los Angeles, but instead went fishing. Bet he wished he went with the team rather than the disabled list.

MLB Debut: 8/6/83

Last MLB appearance: 9/18/95

Career Stats: 74-75

Teams played for: St. Louis, Philadelphia, Pittsburgh, Toronto

Accolades: World Series champion (1993)

JHONNY PERALTA
Shortstop, Third Base, St. Louis

What: Clam chowder versus potato soup

Where: Local establishment

When: March 2013

Story: Who thought a mistake in ordering a bowl of soup would cause Peralta to miss a game, but that's what happened when he had an allergic reaction to a bowl of clam chowder. He was under the impression that it was potato soup. In the immortal words of the Soup Nazi from a Seinfeld episode, "No soup for you!"

MLB Debut: 6/12/03

Last MLB appearance: 6/6/17

Career Stats: .267, 202 HR, 873 RBI

Teams played for: Cleveland, Detroit, St. Louis

Accolades: 3 times All-Star

Fun Fact: In his first plate appearance with Detroit after being traded from Cleveland, he hit a home run.

Chicago Cubs

SAMMY SOSA

Right Field, Chicago Cubs

What: Gesundheit! Story II

Where: San Diego

When: 5/17/2004

Story: Slammin' Sammy sneezed so hard that he sprained a liga-ment in his lower back. The two violent sneezes, apparently caused by back spasms, sent Sosa to the disabled list. The sarcastic side of me says that if he wasn't pumped with all that gym candy, this might not have occurred. On the other hand, because he was on the juice, his recovery should have been quicker than normal!

Teams played for: Texas, Chicago White Sox, Chicago Cubs, Baltimore, Texas

MLB Debut: 6/16/89

Last MLB appearance: 9/29/07

Career Stats: The below stats are all tainted because no one is certain when Swingin' Sammy started with the steroids.

.273, 2,408 H, 609 HR, 1,667 RBI

Accolades: 7 times All-Star, NL MVP (1998), 6 times Silver Slugger Award, NL Hank Aaron Award (1999), Roberto Clem-ente Award (1998), 2 times NL home run leader, 2 times NL RBI leader

Fun Fact: Hit his first career home run came off of Roger Clem-ens.

JOSE CARDENAL
Outfield, Chicago Cubs

What: Do I hear crickets?

Where: Undisclosed hotel, Scottsdale, Arizona

When: Spring 1973

The 1970's afro

Story: Cardenal missed a game during Spring Training in 1973 because he claimed he did not get a good night's sleep due to crickets keeping him up all night!

On opening day 1974, he missed the first game of the year because he slept wrong and one of his eyelids were swollen shut when he woke up. Needless to say, Jose must be a light sleeper.

MLB Debut: 4/14/63

Last MLB Appearance: 10/3/80

Teams played for: San Francisco, California Angels, Cleveland, St. Louis, Milwaukee, Chicago Cubs, Philadelphia, New York Mets, Kansas City

Career Stats: .275, 138 HR, 775 RBI, 1,913 H, 46 3B, 329 SB

Fun Fact: He was one of the last Cuban baseball players to leave Cuba before the Castro regime made it more difficult for players to play outside the island country.

CARLOS ZAMBRANO

Pitcher, Chicago Cubs

What: Pick up the phone, my friend

Where: Zambrano house

When: 2005

Story: I'm all for staying in touch with family, but Zambrano created a ceiling of expectations that not even Paul the Apostle could live up to. As the story goes, Big Z was emailing his brother for four hours a day! You read right, four hours a day. Couldn't he have picked up the phone and given him a call? Was there long distance involved? Needless to say, he experienced elbow soreness.

MLB Debut: 8/20/01

Last MLB appearance: 9/21/12

Teams played for: Chicago Cubs, Miami

Career Stats: 132-91, 3.66 ERA, 1,637 K

Accolades: 3 times All-Star; 3 times Silver Slugger Award, NL wins leader (2006)

Fun Fact: Pitched a no-hitter on 9/14/08.

Fun Fact #2: Became the first player from Venezuela to lead the National League in wins, which he did in 2006.

Fun Fact #3: His 24 career home runs is the most by a Cubs pitcher. He was a switch hitter with a career .238 batting average and 71 RBIs.

MIKE REMLINGER

Pitcher, Chicago Cubs

What: The Remlinger Chair

Where: Cubs clubhouse

When: 5/22/05

Story: Remlinger was relaxing in a reclining chair when he leaned back, pinched his pinkie finger on his pitching hand on another chair next to him, and landed on the disabled list. At the time this injury occurred, Remlinger was pitching poorly, which prompted Cubs broadcaster Steve Stone to mention that players who are playing poorly sit in the Remlinger chair.

Remlinger is a lefty.

MLB Debut: 6/15/91

Last MLB appearance: 6/26/06

Career Stats: 53-55, 3.90 ERA, 854 K

Teams played for: San Francisco, New York Mets, Cincinnati, Atlanta, Chicago Cubs, Boston, Atlanta.

Accolades: All-Star (2002)

RYAN DEMPSTER

Pitcher, Chicago Cubs

What: Watch that step, it's a doozy

Where: Chicago

When: July 2009

Story: As the Cubs celebrated a win, Dempster was fired up to join the celebration, but as he attempted to hop over the dugout railing, he caught his back leg on the railing. When he landed, he fractured his right big toe, which landed him on the disabled list.

Even the kid caught this act of gracefulness!

MLB Debut: 5/23/98

Last MLB appearance: 9/29/13

Career Stats: 132-133, 4.35 ERA, 2,075 K, 87 SV

Teams played for: Florida, Cincinnati, Chicago Cubs, Texas, Boston

Accolades: 2 times All-Star, World Series champion (2013)

Fun Fact: He is the only Cub and one of just three players ever to start a game and collect 30 saves in the same season.

Fun Fact #2: Dempster is tied with the most grand slams allowed in the regular season, with 11. If you include the post-season, move that mark to 12.

KYLE FARNSWORTH
Pitcher, Chicago Cubs

What: Don't kick the fan on a hot day!

Where: Wrigley Field

When: 8/27/04

Story: Apparently after giving up six runs in the ninth inning, Farnsworth had quite enough and took it out on an innocent electric fan. As he kicked it, he sprained his right knee and went on the 15-day disabled list.

Another story involving Farnsworth occurred in June 2009 as a member of the Kansas City Royals. It seems two of his American bulldogs got into a fight. As he was trying to break it up, his hand was bitten and the cuts were deep enough to get close to a tendon. Fortunately, it was his non-throwing hand.

MLB Debut: 4/29/99

Last MLB appearance: 6/25/14

Career Stats: 43-66, 4.26 ERA, 963 K

Teams played for: Chicago Cubs, Detroit, Atlanta, New York Yankees, Detroit, Kansas City, Atlanta, Tampa Bay, Pittsburgh, New York Mets, Houston.

Fun Fact: On 10/1/00 he was the winning pitcher for the final baseball game at Three Rivers Stadium

Fun Fact #2: After retirement, he played amateur football for the Orlando Phantoms for two seasons.

DEREK LEE

First Base, Chicago Cubs

What: Watch the head

Where: San Francisco

When: 9/25/09

Story: After scoring ahead of Jeff Baker, whose go ahead two-run homer in the 9th inning put the Cubs in line for the win, Lee was mobbed by teammates. One in particular, Angel Guzman, was so pumped, he smacked the side of Lee's batting helmet, causing neck spasms. Lee missed five games because of the slap.

On a separate occurrence, Lee was grabbing a bite to eat and went to sit down, only to have the chair collapse, hurting his back.

MLB Debut: 4/28/97

Last MLB appearance: 9/28/11

Career Stats: .281, 331 HR, 1,078 RBI

Teams played for: San Diego, Florida, Chicago Cubs, Atlanta, Baltimore, Pittsburgh

Accolades: 2 times All-Star, World Series champion (2003), 3 times Gold Glove Award, Silver Slugger Award (2005), NL batting champion (2005)

MIKE HARKEY

Pitcher, Chicago Cubs

What: Leave the cartwheels to the pros

Where: Wrigley Field

When: 9/6/92

Story: Somehow during pregame warmups, Harkey had the bright idea to attempt a cartwheel in the outfield, only he didn't land well and severely damaged his knee.

MLB Debut: 9/5/88

Last MLB appearance: 9/28/97

Career Stats: 36-36, 4.49 ERA, 316 K

Teams played for: Chicago Cubs, Colorado, Oakland, California, Los Angeles

ALFONSO SORIANO
Second Base, Left Field, Chicago Cubs

What: Hop hop hopping away to the disabled list

Where: Chicago

When: April 2007

Story: Alfonso had a habit of doing a bunny hop while catching fly balls, only this time he ended up with a strained calf from attempting the hop. That landed him on the 15-day disabled list.

MLB Debut: 9/14/99

Last MLB appearance: 7/5/14

Career Stats: .270, 412 HR, 1,159 RBI, 2,095 H

Teams played for: New York Yankees, Texas Rangers, Washington, Chicago Cubs, New York Yankees

Accolades: 7 times All-Star, 4 times Silver Slugger Award, AL stolen base leader (2002)

Fun Fact: One of only four players in the 40-40 club—40 home runs and 40 stolen bases in one season.

Fun Fact #2: Is only the third player to start All-Star games for both leagues at two different positions.

Fun Fact #3: In 2006, became the first outfielder player in baseball history with 40 home runs, 40 stolen bases, and 20 assists.

Cincinnati Reds

STEVE FOSTER

Pitcher, Cincinnati

What: Warm up first

Where: The Jay Leno Show

When: 1993

Story: Foster was invited to The Tonight Show with Jay Leno. During a segment of throwing baseballs at milk bottles, he injured his shoulder. That landed him on the disabled list with inflammation in his shoulder. He retired that year.

MLB Debut: 8/22/91

Last MLB appearance: 6/26/93

Career Stats: 3-3, 2.41 ERA, 61 K

Teams played for: Cincinnati

JOHN VANDER WAL

Outfield, First Base, Cincinnati

What: Hire a young whipper snapper to do the job, John

Where: Michigan

When: Winter 2004

Story: Before the 2004 season, Vander Wal blew out his knee shoveling snow. After that unfortunate event, he only appeared in 42 games for the Reds that season, which turned out to be his last one in the big leagues.

MLB Debut: 9/6/91

Last MLB appearance: 9/27/04

Career Stats: .261, 97 HR, 430 RBI

Teams played for: Montreal, Colorado, San Diego, Pittsburgh, San Francisco, New York Yankees, Milwaukee, Cincinnati

Fun Fact: Holds the record of pinch hits in a season, with 28 in 1995.

Pittsburgh Pirates

AJ Burnett   205

AJ BURNETT
Pitcher, Pittsburgh

What: Bunt with the bat, not your face, AJ!

Where: Bradenton, Florida

When: 3/1/12

Story: Burnett was taking pregame batting practice when the ball ricocheted, not on the ground like a batted ball is supposed to, but onto his face, resulting in a broken orbital bone. Burnett did not make his debut with the Pirates until later in April.

MLB Debut: 8/17/99

Last MLB appearance: 10/3/15

Career Stats: 164-157, 3.99 ERA, 2,513 K

Teams played for: Florida, Toronto, New York Yankees, Pittsburgh, Philadelphia, Pittsburgh.

Accolades: All-Star (2015), World Series champion (2003 and 2009), AL strikeout leader (2008)

Fun Fact: Pitched a no-hitter on 5/12/01.

Fun Fact #2: While warming up for a start on 9/7/01, Burnett threw a warm-up pitch that accidentally struck the window of a moving pickup truck. In the immortal words of Harry Doyle, "Just a bit outside."

Fun Fact #3: On 6/20/09, while pitching for the Yankees and ironically against his former team, the Marlins, struck out three batters on nine pitches. That, my friends, is called an immaculate inning.

San Francisco Giants

MICHAEL MORSE
Outfield, First Base, Shortstop, San Francisco

Morse is the third player on the right.

What: Two heads collide = one big headache

Where: Oracle Park, San Francisco

When: 5/29/17

Story: It was a beautiful 58-degree day in May, with the Nationals leading the Giants 2-0. Hunter Strickland, who is still hacked that Bryce Harper hit 2 home runs off of him in the 2014 playoffs almost 3 years ago, promptly sends a fastball that hits Harper. As words are exchanged, helmets are flying and so are the punches. Michael Morse comes running in to help out. (How do you help out in a bench-clearing brawl, by the way?) He collides with his teammate Jeff Samardzija and with that collision, Morse lands on the 10-day disabled list.

Morse was put on the 7-day concussion list and never played in another major league game.

MLB Debut: 5/31/05

Last MLB appearance: 5/29/17

Career Stats: .274, 105 HR, 355 RBI

Teams played for: Seattle, Washington, Seattle, Baltimore, San Francisco, Miami, Pittsburgh, San Francisco

Accolades: 2014 World Series Champion

MADISON BUMGARNER
Pitcher, San Francisco

How am I going to explain this to management?

What: Dirt bike accident

Where: Denver, CO

When: 4/22/17

Story: The Giants ace missed nearly two months of the 2017 season after a dirt bike accident during one of the team's scheduled off days in Denver. Bumgarner, who'd been riding dirt bikes his whole life, rented a bike and went out riding in the mountains. He bruised some ribs and sprained his pitching shoulder in the crash. Madison was put on the disabled list in April and did not return until mid-July.

I'm willing to bet that his contract had some sort of language prohibiting him from riding dirt bikes on his off day.

Bumgarner is a lefty.

MLB Debut: 9/8/09

Teams played for: San Francisco

Career Stats: 119-92, 3.13 ERA, 1,794 K, hit 17 career home runs, including 2 grand slams which tied a major league record.

 Accolades: 3 times World Series Champion (2010, 2012, 2014) and 4 times All-Star

JEREMY AFFELDT
Pitcher, San Francisco

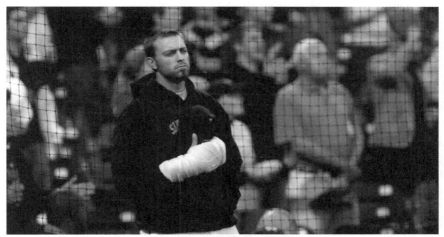

Man, could have sworn those burgers were thawed!

— STORY I —

What: Thaw first before cutting burgers

Where: His home

When: 9/8/11

Story: Giants reliever Jeremy Affeldt was done for the season after sustaining a deep cut in his right hand while using a knife to separate frozen burger patties. The cut was so severe that it caused nerve damage and came within a millimeter of an artery. It required 8 hours of surgery. Manager Bruce Bochy called it an "unfortunate accident."

Affeldt is a lefty.

MLB Debut: 4/6/02

Last appearance: 10/4/15

Teams played for: Kansas City, Colorado, Cincinnati, and San Francisco

Career Stats: 43-46, 3.97 ERA; 720 K

Accolades: 3 times World Series Champion (2010, 2012, 2014)

—STORY II—

What: "Happy you're home"

Where: Affeldt house

When: 2012

Story: Affeldt landed on the 15-day disabled list after his son leaped off the sofa and ran into his arms, only to strain the medial collateral ligament in his right knee.

—STORY III—

What: Lake play time

Where: Loon Lake, Spokane, Washington

When: 2015

Story: While celebrating his son's birthday party at Loon Lake, he slipped off the platform and injured his knee—again. Diagnosed as a subluxated knee, he landed some time on the disabled list for that one.

—STORY IV—

What: Ah-Choo

Where: On the road

When: 2013

Story: Lying in bed, he began to sneeze quite heavily. The next thing you know, he strains an oblique from sneezing too hard.

CHRIS BROWN
Third Base, San Francisco

What: The sandman taketh

Where: Dominican League

Story: Brown missed a game with a strained eyelid after sleeping on it in a funny way.

MLB Debut: 9/3/84

Last MLB appearance: 5/16/89

Career Stats: .269, 38 HR, 184 RBI

Teams played for: San Francisco, San Diego, Detroit

Accolades: All-Star (1986)

Fun Fact: High School teammate of Darryl Strawberry.

MATT CAIN
Pitcher, San Francisco

What: That knife will bite!

Where: At the ballpark

When: April 2014

Story: How to catch a knife. If you're Matt Cain, not with the handle. Seems that Matt cut the tip of his right index finger after he arrived at the ballpark. When Cain was in the kitchen, he dropped the knife as he was trying to cut the sandwiches into fancy triangles. He cut his finger as he tried to catch the knife. Ouch! Hey Matt, leave the fancy cutting to the moms!

MLB Debut: 8/29/05

Last MLB Appearance: 9/30/17

Teams played for: San Francisco

Career Stats: 104-118, 3.68 ERA, 1,694 K

Accolades: 3 times All-Star, 2 times World Series Champion (2010, 2012)

Fun Fact: Pitched a perfect game on 6/13/12 which coincidentally was on the same day my boys (Andrew and Jaren) turned 10.

KEVIN MITCHELL
Left Field, San Francisco

What: Gold filling

Where: His house

When: March 1990

Story: Kevin was hungry for a sugar rush one morning when he came across a frozen donut. Not wanting it to thaw at room temperature, Mitchell did the only common sense thing: to microwave that sucker. Not only did he burn his tongue and the roof of his mouth, but the molten frosting made its way through the cracks in his fillings—resulting in Mitchell needing to get at least one root canal.

I'm no economics expert, but hey, that is one expensive donut!

MLB Debut: 9/4/84

Last MLB appearance: 8/3/98

Teams played for: New York Mets, San Diego, San Francisco, Seattle, Cincinnati, Boston, Cincinnati, Cleveland, Oakland

Career Stats: .284, 234 HR, 760 RBI

Accolades: 2 times All-Star, World Series Champion (1986), NL MVP (1989), Silver Slugger (1989), NL Home Run leader (1989)

Fun Fact: Mitchell is the only player to win a Most Valuable Player award and play for five major league teams before his 32nd birthday.

RON BRYANT
Pitcher, San Francisco

What: Heads up!

Where: Spring Training

When: 3/15/74

Story: Bryant severely cut his side while diving into a swimming pool. He won only four more games the rest of the year and his career was never the same.

Bryant is a lefty.

MLB debut: 9/29/67

Last MLB appearance: 7/29/75

Career Stats: 57-56, 4.02 ERA, 509 K

Teams played for: San Francisco, St. Louis

Accolades: NL wins leader (1973)

Fun Fact: 1973 *Sporting News* pitcher of the year.

JEFF KENT
Second Base, San Francisco

What: Washing truck or riding his motorcycle, which is it Jeff?

Where: Kent's property

When: 3/1/02

Story: The truth really does come out eventually. Seems that Jeff's story of washing his truck did not match the fact that eyewitnesses saw a man fitting Kent's description doing wheelies on his motorcycle. That would be against his contract to attempt motorcycle stunts. So the broken left wrist came from "washing his truck" not by attempting wheelies and wiping out, as Kent strongly suggested to folks who witnessed this. In the words of Frank Drebin, "Nothing to see here!"

MLB Debut: 4/12/92

Last MLB appearance: 9/27/08

Teams played for: Toronto, New York Mets, Cleveland, San Francisco, Houston, Los Angeles Dodgers

Career Stats: .290, 377 HR, 1,518 RBI, 2,461 H

Accolades: 5 times All-Star, 4 times Silver Slugger, NL MVP (2000), All-time leader in home runs as a second-baseman; only second baseman to have 100 or more RBIs in 6 consecutive seasons (1997-2002).

ROGER METZGER
Shortstop, San Francisco

What: Measure twice, cut once

Where: Brenham, Texas

When: 11/29/79

Story: Metzger was in the process of making a playhouse for his two boys in time for Christmas when the saw grabbed the wood; the momentum pulled his right hand into the saw blade. The tips of the four fingers were sliced off, including up to the first knuckle on his index finger. He attempted a comeback with the Giants but was released later in the 1980 season.

MLB Debut: 6/16/70

Last MLB appearance: 8/10/80

Career Stats: .231, 5 HR, 254 RBI

Teams played for: Chicago Cubs, Houston, San Francisco

Accolades: Gold Glove Award (1973)

BRETT TOMKO
Pitcher, San Francisco

What: Dancing with Tomko

Where: San Francisco

When: 9/1/04

Story: Tomko was so pumped after striking out Royce Clayton of the Rockies that he did a pirouette; he did not land well and sprained his ankle.

With as many teams Brett played for, he had better have been a renter!

MLB Debut: 5/27/97

Last MLB appearance: 5/24/11

Career Stats: 100-103, 4.65 ERA, 1,209 K

Teams played for: Cincinnati, Seattle, San Diego, St. Louis, San Francisco, Los Angeles, San Diego, Kansas City, San Diego, New York Yankees, Oakland, Texas

Fun Fact: Was one of the four players involved in the trade that brought Ken Griffey Jr. from Seattle to Cincinnati.

Fun Fact #2: Tomko's father won a contest of over 11,000 entries for naming the Cleveland Cavaliers NBA team in 1970.

KEIICHI YABU

Pitcher, San Francisco

What: Ricochet

Where: San Francisco clubhouse

When: April 2008

Story: While using an exercise band to strengthen his arms, they snapped loose and struck him in the face, scratching both corneas and causing blurred vision for a few days.

MLB Debut: 4/9/05

Last MLB appearance: 9/27/08

Career Stats: 7-6, 4.00 ERA, 92 K

Teams played for: Oakland, San Francisco

FREDDIE FITZSIMMONS
Pitcher, New York Giants

What: Chairs that prove to be dangerous

Where: New York

When: 1927

Story: Apparently, rocking chairs can be quite dangerous. Fat Freddie was falling asleep when he crushed his fingers underneath the chair as he chatted with Rogers Hornsby and Bill Terry. His absence from the lineup may have cost the '27 Giants the pennant.

MLB Debut: 8/12/25

Last MLB appearance: 6/16/43

Career Stats: 217-146, 3.51 ERA, 870 K

Teams played for: New York Giants, Brooklyn Dodgers

Team's manager and/or coach: Philadelphia, Brooklyn, Boston Braves, New York Giants, Chicago Cubs, Kansas City Athletics, Chicago Cubs.

Accolades: 2 times World Series champion (1933 as a player for the New York Giants and 1954 as a coach for the Giants).

DUSTAN MOHR

Outfield, San Francisco

What: Check twice, step once

Where: San Diego

When: September 2004

Story: Mohr hurt his leg falling over the visitor's bullpen mound while catching the game-winning sacrifice fly. An MRI exam in San Francisco revealed no damage to any of the ligaments but a bad bruise to the back of the kneecap.

MLB Debut: 8/29/01

Last MLB Appearance: 7/8/07

Career Stats: .249, 49 HR, 156 RBI

Teams played for: Minnesota, San Francisco, Colorado, Boston, Tampa Bay

Los Angeles Dodgers

JOE KELLY
Pitcher, Los Angeles Dodgers

What: Cajun cooking

Where: Phoenix, Arizona

When: Spring Training 2019

Story: Kelly wanted to do some home cooking for his Dodgers teammates. The only problem with that is he stayed hunched over a stove for five hours! His back tightened up and missed his next scheduled start. Sure hope the crawfish was worth it!

MLB Debut: 6/10/12

Career Stats: 48-29, 3.92 ERA, 560 K

Teams played for: St. Louis, Boston, Los Angeles

Accolades: World Series champion (2018)

JOSH REDDICK
Outfield, Los Angeles Dodgers

What: Flipping the bird to the door doesn't always work

Where: Unknown Hotel

When: August 2016

Story: There are a number of ways a baseball player might injure a finger. Ordering room service at a hotel isn't traditionally one of them. Reddick hurt a finger while holding his door open for a room service cart. He was scratched from the lineup because of discomfort he experienced while throwing a ball.

MLB Debut: 7/31/09

Teams played for: Boston, Oakland, Los Angeles Dodgers, Houston

Career Stats: .263, 140 HR, 531 RBI

Accolades: World Series Champion (2017)

A.J. ELLIS
Catcher, Los Angeles Dodgers

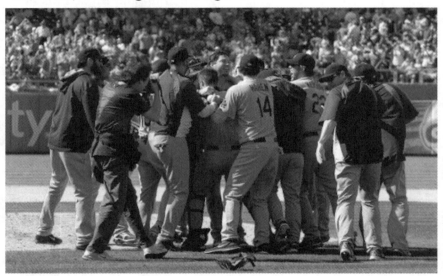

Guys, who put that mask there?

What: Be careful where you step

Where: Philadelphia

When: 5/25/14

Story: The 24th career no-hitter in the Los Angeles Dodgers history proved to be quite painful for AJ.

Ellis went on the 15-day disabled list with a sprained right ankle, a day after getting hurt while celebrating Josh Beckett's no-hitter. Ellis rushed to join his teammates in the celebration Sunday in Philadelphia. Around home plate, he stepped on the discarded mask of backup Drew Butera.

Watch that step AJ, it's a doozy!

MLB Debut: 9/15/08

Last MLB appearance: 9/30/18

Teams played for: Los Angeles Dodgers, Philadelphia, Miami, San Diego

Career Stats: .239, 44 HR, 229 RBI

Fun Fact: He is from the same hometown, Cape Girardeau, Missouri, as Rush Limbaugh.

RALPH ONIS
Catcher, Brooklyn Dodgers

What: Was the sandwich worth it?

Where: Tinker Field, Jacksonville, FL

When: Spring Training 1935

Story: Ralph bit into a sandwich so hard that he dislocated his jaw. That bite kept him sidelined for a while, but he came back in April to collect a single in his only major league at bat.

MLB Debut: 4/27/35

Last MLB appearance: 4/27/35

Career Stats: 1.000 (1-1)

Teams played for: Brooklyn

San Diego Padres

ADAM EATON
Pitcher, San Diego

What: "Put the knife down, Adam before someone gets hurt... like you."

Where: His house

When: 6/1/01

Story: Unable to unwrap the plastic sealing by hand that held his Happy Gilmore and Backdraft DVDs together, Eaton resorted to a knife that he got from his grandfather for Christmas. The good news is that he tore open the plastic. The bad news is that he wasn't able to watch the movie right away because as he opened up the plastic covering the movie, he somehow stabbed himself in the stomach, which resulted in an ambulance ride to the local hospital and a response from the ER asking if he had done this on purpose.

Adam has been put on a ban by his family from using any sharp objects.

MLB Debut: 5/30/00

Last MLB appearance: 8/24/09

Teams played for: San Diego, Texas, Philadelphia, Baltimore, Colorado

Career Stats: 71-68, 4.94 ERA, 855 K

Accolades: World Series Champion (2008)

JAY WITASICK
Pitcher, San Diego

What: Heavier than you think

Where: Witasick residence

When: Spring 2003

Story: This is not your usual story of straining a tendon in the elbow. Seems that Jay was throwing away a trash bag full of watermelon rinds, when he ended up hurting his elbow. He only appeared in 46 games that season.

MLB Debut: 7/7/96

Last MLB appearance: 9/26/07

Career Stats: 32-41, 4.64 ERA, 645 K

Teams played for: Oakland, Kansas City, San Diego, New York Yankees, San Francisco, San Diego, Colorado, Oakland, Tampa Bay

MILTON BRADLEY
Outfield, San Diego

Let me up, I wasn't done arguing!

What: Temper temper

Where: San Diego

When: 9/23/07

Story: After running out a play to first base, Bradley had an exchange with first base umpire Mike Winters. The argument quickly got heated, and as Bradley was held back by manager Bud Black, he got his leg tangled with Black and tore his ACL. He missed the remainder of the season, including the one game playoff with Colorado.

Upon investigation, it was found that Winters actually instigated the exchange and Bradley was not suspended.

MLB Debut: 7/19/00

Last MLB appearance: 5/8/11

Career Stats: .271, 125 HR, 481 RBI

Teams played for: Montreal, Cleveland, Los Angeles Dodgers, Oakland, San Diego, Texas, Chicago, Seattle

Accolades: All-Star (2008)

Fun Fact: For Oakland in 2006, he became one of three players ever to have hit a home run on each side of the plate in a post-season game.

MAT LATOS
Pitcher, San Diego

What: Let it go, Mat

Where: Denver

When: July 2010

Story: Latos was walking down the steps at Coors Field. Instead of letting go a sneeze, like numerous other stories in this book, Latos held in the sneeze, which ended up causing pain in his side. This, in turn, led the Padres to put him on the 15-day disabled list.

MLB Debut: 7/19/09

Teams played for: San Diego, Cincinnati, Miami, Los Angeles Dodgers, Los Angeles Angels, Chicago White Sox, Washington, Toronto

Career Stats: 71-59, 3.64 ERA, 1,011 K

AKINORA OTSUKA
Pitcher, San Diego

What: Bat or paper

Where: San Diego

When: 2004

Story: Otsuka was signing autographs when he noticed a piece of paper and a bat coming at him at the same time. He took his eyes off the bat, which was a bad idea, and glanced at the paper. Next thing you know, he got hit in the face with that flying bat. One would think that if you had to pick between what is flying at you, a bat or a piece of paper, you'd pick the bat. Not Akinora!

MLB Debut: 4/6/04

Last MLB appearance: 7/1/07

Career Stats: 13-15, 2.44 ERA, 217 K, 39 SV

Teams played for: San Diego, Texas

DAVID WELLS

Pitcher, San Diego Story II

What: Flip-flops versus iron barstool, round 1

Where: Wells kitchen

When: 5/20/04

Story: The moral of this story is not to slap David. It seems that one of his buddies came up from behind him and slapped him on the neck, which Wells did not take kindly to. So he attempted to kick a wrought-iron barstool, weighing between 30 and 40 pounds, while wearing flip-flops I might add. The story gets a whole lot better as Wells trips after kicking the barstool, loses his balance, and falls head first over the bar stool. He then lands on a bottle of wine, cuts his right arm with the bottle, and ends up on the disabled list to repair a tendon he cut in the fracas.

MLB appearance: 6/30/87

Last MLB appearance: 9/28/07

Teams played for: Toronto, Detroit, Cincinnati, Baltimore, New York Yankees, Toronto, Chicago White Sox, New York Yankees, San Diego, Boston, San Diego, Los Angeles Dodgers

Career Stats: 239-147, 4.13 ERA, 2,201 K

Accolades: 3 times All-Star, 2 times World Series champion, AL wins leader in 2000

Fun Fact: Pitched a perfect game 5/17/98.

Hooray, the hangover is gone!

Fun Fact #2: He attended the same high school as Don Larsen, whose perfect game for the Yankees in the 1956 World Series was the only one ever pitched in post-season.

Fun Fact #3: On 9/28/03, the final game of the regular season, Wells earned the 200th win of his career in a game managed by Roger Clemens.

Fun Fact #4: Appeared in the post-season with six different teams, tying Kenny Lofton for the most all-time.

TONY GWYNN
Right Field, San Diego

What: Watch that door

Where: San Diego

Story: Gwynn smashed his thumb in the door of his luxury car while on his way to the bank which caused him to miss a couple of games. I'm sure that deposit was well worth it.

MLB Debut: 7/19/82

Last MLB appearance: 10/7/01

Career Stats: .338, 3,141 H, 135 HR, 1,138 RBI

Teams played for: San Diego

Accolades: 8 times NL batting champion, 15 times All-Star, 5 times Gold Glove Award, 7 times Silver Slugger Award

First-ballot Hall of Famer–2007

Fun Fact: Won eight batting titles, tied for the most in National League history.

Fun Fact #2: He was an all-conference athlete in both baseball and basketball at San Diego State, becoming the only player in the history of the WAC to accomplish that feat.

Fun Fact #3: Gwynn's son, Tony Gwynn Jr., whose major league debut (with the Milwaukee Brewers) and first major league hit on 7/19/06, came 24 years to the day of his father's first major league hit—each Gwynn hit a double.

Fun Fact #4: Gwynn never hit below .309 in a full season.

Fun Fact #5: In the 1987 Padres home opener, Marvell Wynne, Gwynn, and John Kruk hit back-to-back-to-back homers to start the season. This was the first time a team had led off a game with 3 consecutive home runs.

Fun Fact #6: He reached 3,000 hits in 2,284 games, the third-fewest to reach the mark behind Ty Cobb and Nap Lajoie.

JUSTIN HATCHER
Bullpen Catcher, San Diego

What: That rascally rodent

Where: Colorado

When: May 2011

Story: It seems there was a lot of action before the game preluding a very exciting 9-7 Padres victory over the Rockies. Somehow a squirrel got into the bullpen and as several coaches tried to shoo him away, Hatcher grabbed the little guy. As he dropped him, the squirrel bit him a couple of times on his thumb, thus requiring a couple of penicillin shots.

TAGG BOZIED
First Base, San Diego prospect

7/29/04. After hitting a game-winning grand slam in the minor leagues, he leaped into the air, landed on home plate, and ruptured his patellar tendon. Needless to say, he was out the rest of the year. He played for several minor league teams, but never made it to the majors.

Colorado Rockies

GREG HOLLAND
Pitcher, Colorado

What: This man was not made for the kitchen

Where: Holland house

When: August 2017

Story: Holland was day-to-day following a kitchen accident involving cutting his index finger—presumably helping out with the dishes. Let's just say that helping out with the dishes should only be done in the off-season for Greg.

What made matters worse is that he was leading the majors in saves.

MLB Debut: 8/2/10

Teams played for: Kansas City, Colorado, St. Louis, Washington, Arizona

Career Stats: 24-22, 2.96 ERA, 588 K, 206 SV

Accolades: 3 Times All-Star

World Series Champion (2015), AL Reliever of the Year (2014)

NL Saves leader (2017); NL Comeback player of the Year (2017)

JOSH OUTMAN
Pitcher, Colorado

What: Smell it before you taste it

Where: Denny's (America's Diner)

When: 4/4/12

MLB Debut: 9/2/08

Story: Rule number 1 in eating food: If it doesn't pass the smell test, it doesn't pass the eating test. Who cooked for Josh? Needless to say, that individual will not be cooking for Josh anytime soon and/or that restaurant will not be visited anytime in the foreseeable future! Man, makes me almost sick when you think about how hard he was "exhaling the food." Gives new meaning to "spewing out of your mouth!"

From that experience, Outman strained his oblique because of the excessive vomiting brought on by food poisoning.

Teams played for: Oakland, Colorado, Cleveland, New York Yankees

Career Stats: 16-11, 4.43 ERA, 226 K

JEREMY GUTHRIE
Pitcher, Colorado

What: You never forget about riding a bike—or do you?

Where: Colorado

When: April 2013

Story: Guthrie was getting some cardio in as he was riding his bike to the ballpark when the chain on his bike broke off. He fell off the bike, jammed his shoulder, and then was put on the 15-day disabled list.

MLB Debut: 8/28/04

Last MLB appearance: 4/8/17

Career Stats: 91-109, 4.42 ERA, 1,046 K

Teams played for: Cleveland, Baltimore, Colorado, Kansas City, Washington

CLINT BARMES
Second Base and Shortstop, Colorado

What: Expensive trip to the grocery store—I meant carrying deer meat for a teammate

Where: Barmes' apartment

When: 6/5/05

Story: Through the first two months of the 2005 season, it looked as if Barmes was the frontrunner for the NL Rookie of the Year Award. And then he went food shopping, or so he said.

Barmes walked up the stairs, carrying a bag of groceries in one arm and a sweatshirt in the other.

He slipped on the steps, dropped the sweatshirt and landed on his shoulder, breaking his collarbone.

The following day, Barmes came clean—it wasn't groceries that he was lugging up the stairs, but a package of deer meat that he received from teammate Todd Helton when he crashed to the ground and broke his left collarbone.

Barmes would miss nearly three months of the season, and he'd finish eighth in the NL Rookie of the Year voting.

What's interesting about this injury is that for the first 86 games of his career, Barmes batted .318. However, after the injury and 579 games later, he batted .244. Quite a dramatic difference!

MLB appearance: 9/5/03

Last MLB appearance: 10/4/15

Teams played for: Colorado, Houston, Pittsburgh, San Diego

Career Stats: .245, 89 HR, 415 RBI

Arizona Diamondbacks

IAN KENNEDY

Pitcher, Arizona

What: Extreme dishwashing

Where: Kennedy house

When: 5/27/13

Story: Whoever thought that doing the dishes could turn into such a bloody affair? Well, that's what Ian found out when he decided to help with the dishes at the Kennedy house. Seems he cut his hand on a knife which caused him to miss a start. Bet he thinks twice about helping out in the kitchen next time he is asked, especially during the season!

MLB Debut: 9/1/07

Teams played for: New York Yankees, Arizona, San Diego, Kansas City

Career Stats: 97-103, 4.09 ERA, 1,633 K and 30 SV

Accolades: NL wins leader (2011)

BRIAN ANDERSON

Pitcher, Arizona

What: Costly cab ride

Where: Arizona

When: July 1998

Story: Anderson suffered nerve damage in his elbow after a cab ride in Beverly Hills. He laid his pitching arm across the top of the back seat for the 20-minute ride. That night he felt stiffness in his elbow. When he tried to throw, he almost had no range of motion.

That is one expensive cab ride, partly because he was going shopping on Rodeo Drive.

Other such experiences with Anderson are: During spring training one year, Anderson forgot his hat, spikes, and glove and had to visit a nearby Walmart, where he bought a softball glove for $30. Coincidentally, he got three comebackers to the mound in an inning! Since he was endorsing Rawlings, he had to black out the glove's Wilson label and Adidas stripes on the spikes.

In 2003, he and a teammate chased down and caught a purse thief who had stolen a purse in a restaurant near their hotel. The pitchers took the thief back, returned the purse, and held the knucklehead for police.

While trying to remove a jammed atomizer plunger from a cologne bottle, he cut the middle finger of his pitching hand.

How about this one: He once burned his face ironing, while watching a baseball game. He picked up the iron, held it to his face to feel the heat and was attempting to look around the corner (of the iron) to watch the game. Well, his cheek got in the way and it didn't take much to fry the side of his face.

And lastly, Anderson sleepwalked naked out of his hotel room at 4:30 a.m. He went down to the elevators looking for a house phone, but there was none. He took a newspaper to cover up as much as he could before he could snag a towel from the workout room. Not sure if anyone caught a glimpse of him in his birthday suit!

Anderson is a lefty.

MLB Debut: 9/10/93

Last MLB appearance: 5/8/05

Career Stats: 82-83, 4.74 ERA, 723 K

Teams played for: California, Cleveland, Arizona, Cleveland, Kansas City

Accolades: World Series champion (2001)

MARK GRACE

First Baseman, Arizona

What: Celebration gone awry

Where: Arizona clubhouse

When: Summer 2002

Story: It seems that Grace was so pumped up that teammate Damian Miller made the All-Star team, that as he came across the clubhouse to congratulate him, he slammed his toe against a couch and broke it.

MLB Debut: 5/2/88

Last MLB appearance: 9/28/03

Career Stats: .303, 173 HR, 1,146 RBI, 2,445 H

Teams played for: Chicago Cubs, Arizona

Accolades: 3 times All-Star, 4 times Gold Glove Award, World Series champion (2001)

Fun Fact: During the 1990's, led the major leagues in hits and doubles.

CARLOS BAERGA

Second Base, Arizona

What: Unleaded or Diesel?

Where: Gas station

When: 2003

Story: Baerga cut his finger when he handed money over to his cousin to pay for gas and got his hand slammed in the door.

MLB Debut: 4/14/90

Last MLB appearance: 9/30/05

Career Stats: .291, 134 HR, 774 RBI

Teams played for: Cleveland, New York Mets, San Diego, Cleveland, Boston, Arizona, Washington

Accolades: 3 times All-Star, 2 times Silver Slugger Award

Fun Fact: In 1992-93 became the first second baseman since 1922 to have back-to-back 200 plus hits, 20 plus HR, 100 plus RBI and a .300 plus average.

Fun Fact #2: On 4/8/93 he became the first player in major league history to hit a home run from both sides of the plate in the same inning.

PLAYERS

A

B

C

TEAMS